FEMALE RITUAL SERVITUDE

The Trokosis in Ghana

WISDOM YAW MENSAH

AND FRANCIS EBENEZER GODWYLL

authorHOUSE®

AuthorHouse™
1663 Liberty Drive
Bloomington, IN 47403
www.authorhouse.com
Phone: 1-800-839-8640

First published by AuthorHouse 1/5/2010

ISBN: 978-1-4389-4949-9 (sc)

Printed in the United States of America
Bloomington, Indiana

This book is printed on acid-free paper.

TABLE OF CONTENTS

INTRODUCTION

THROUGHOUT HISTORY, WOMEN AND CHILDREN have suffered various forms of violence, discrimination, and mistreatment from individuals and societies. They have become the most vulnerable group in the world, consistently facing acts of violence, including sex trafficking, slavery, rape, domestic violence, and objectification of their bodies. There are other forms of cold-blooded and brutal treatment of women and children that have persisted even in the twenty-first century. Since these acts of violence against women are situated in the context of culture, human right conventions have not always been effective in responding to them.

While the agenda to promote the well-being of women has come a long way, there are several heinous practices that linger on in many countries. One of these practices in Ghana is the Trokosi system, practiced largely among the Ewes in Southeastern Ghana. In what frame of mind do family members make the decision to send a virgin girl to a shrine to atone for the sins of another person? Underlying this decision is an assumption of ownership and control. If they did not perceive themselves of having the power and, in actuality, exercising that power over the existence of the female, then they could not have acted that way. In the broader context, is the environment or societal structure that accepts, condones, or looks the other way, when such outrageous and unjustified powers are exercised: In this context the girl is dehumanized, and since she does not have the power to make decisions about her own life choices, she is diminished. A girl could therefore be viewed in this paradigm as the property of the father, the family, the husband, and sometimes the entire village. All or any of whom could exercise control over the life choices of a girl.

In this book we explain how life-altering decisions are made on behalf of innocent virgins who are used to mollify the gods so as to avert a perceived punishment for sins committed by others. Surprisingly, those whose sins are being pacified are sometimes fairly remote from the existence of the "sacrificial lamb" – the girl child. This should not be seen as an isolated phenomenon taking place in the Southeastern corner of Ghana, but rather as part of the bigger picture of the marginalization of females and sometimes the powerlessness of their circumstances. Amnesty International (2002) and DAWN (2003) comment on a practice called *swara* in Pakistan's North West Frontier Province and the tribal territories. The practice involves using young females to settle conflicts with rival partners. Burn (2005) reports of dowry deaths which sometimes occur in India and Pakistan in scenarios where a wife's husband or in-laws may kill her if her family is unable to provide the dowry agreed upon in the event of a divorce. The woman could, in some cases, be held over a cooking stove until her sari catches fire. According to Burn (2005), there were about 7,000 such deaths reported by the Indian government in 2001. These are but a few examples of viewing women as chattels.

We have also characterized the Trokosi system as slavery. Domestic slavery was common in Africa when traditional rulers and men in good economic standing owned slaves. Even though many scholars assert that the scale and callousness that characterized the Trans-Atlantic slave made the abominations of the institution of domestic slavery pale into insignificance, there were still certain norms that depicted the slave as less than human.

Mendosa (2002) articulates two main issues. First the slave could be bought, sold, traded, lent, and, in some states, such as the Asante of Ghana, could be killed for rituals or for large national celebrations. The second issue was that the slave could not sacrifice to his or her ancestors. Upon death he or she was not given a normal funeral but the body could be merely cast into a river or discarded as trash. Thus, the absence of ceremonies to assist living souls to transform into ancestral spirits denies them eternal life. This is to say even in death, they are not supposedly accorded the same status as a free person. The slave–owner–slave relationship can best be described in terms of the dominance of "insiders" who feel legally empowered over "outsiders" who are vulnerable and deprived of even basic human rights. This relationship is not devoid of all forms of violence towards the slaves.

Thus, considering enslavement in a global context, rather than "Atlantic" or American, historical context indicates that many people – often females – entered slavery through nonviolent means, notably because of family indebtedness or for upward social mobility. Joseph Miller's essay emphasizes the growing presence of merchants among the militarists who seized women by sheer violence from ancient times; indeed, debt was possibly the most common cause of enslavement everywhere. Also, fathers, uncles, and other representatives of fundamentally patriarchal communities tended to lessen the problems of caring for the people for whom they were responsible by disposing of the girls and women who bore children in numbers they could not support. In addition natural catastrophes, such as famine, often triggered this defensive strategy of selling girls to save other relatives (Campbell, Miers, & Miller, 2008).

This book seeks to take us through a journey of the lives of innocent virgins who were sent into ritual slavery by their families so as to avert punishment from the gods for sins committed by relatives. By making known their plight through their own voices we are standing in solidarity with the victims of the heinous institution and echoing the words of Dr. Nafis Sadik (1995): "we must be courageous in speaking out about the issues that concern us; we must not bend under the weight of spurious arguments invoking culture or traditional values. No value worth the name supports the oppression and enslavement of women" (par. 12).

We also identify with the words of Mahatma Ghandi: "It is good to swim in the waters of tradition but to sink in them is suicide" (quoted in Brown, 1989, p. 212). The Ewe ethnic group in southeastern portion of Ghana, among whom the Trokosi practice is rife, is a patriarchal society which, like other similar communities, has organized and arranged privileges and roles that place the female at a disadvantage. Gerda Lerner characterizes such societies and likens them to a stage. She writes:

> Men and women live on the stage, on which they act out their assigned roles, equal in importance. The play cannot go on without both performers. Neither of them "contributes" more or less to the whole; neither is marginal or dispensable. But the stage set is conceived, painted, and defined by men. Men have written the play, have directed the show...assigned themselves the most interesting most heroic parts. (cited in Nikolić-Ristanović, 2000, p. 22)

Female Ritual Servitude: The Trokosis in Ghana is divided into seven chapters. Chapter 1 reports agonizing stories of victims of a 300-year-old tradition known in the Republic of Ghana in West Africa as Trokosi. The next chapter gives a brief picture of The Republic of Ghana – a context to the stories so that our readers who are unfamiliar with this land can build some meaningful associations. Chapter 3 explains the Trokosi system and practice in detail. Chapter 4 discusses movements and actions to liberate victims from the Trokosi practice. Rehabilitation efforts of the Trokosi system by individuals and various institutions are discussed in the next chapter. Chapter 6 reviews the roles of the Government of Ghana, NGOs, and the civil society at large in the liberation process. The last chapter analyzes some discourses that influence perspectives on the Trokosi system.

References

Amnesty International. (2002). Pakistan: The tribal justice system in Pakistan. Retrieved August 29, 2008, from http://asiapacific.amnesty.org/library/Index/ENGASA330242002?open&of=ENG-2AS

Brown, J. M. (1989). *Gandhi: Prisoner of hope*. London: Yale University Press.

Burn, S. M. (2005). *Women across cultures: A global perspective*. New York: McGraw-Hill.

Campbell, G., Miers, S., & Miller, J. C. (2008). *Women and slavery: Africa, the Indian Ocean world, and the medieval North Atlantic*. Athens, OH: Ohio University Press.

DAWN. (2003, June 6). Victim of "Swara" custom acquitted: Sentence in murder case overturned. Retrieved August 29, 2008, from http://www.dawn.com/2003/06/06/local28.htm

Mendosa, E. L. (2002). *West Africa: An introduction to its history, civilization and contemporary situation.* Durham, NC: Carolina Academic Press.

Nikolić-Ristanović, V. (2000). *Women, violence and war: Wartime victimization of refugees in the Balkans.* Hungary: Central European University Press.

Sadik, N. (1995). *Madam president, honorable delegates.* Paper presented at the Fourth World Conference on Women, Beijing, China. Retrieved August 29, 2008, from http://www.un.org/esa/gopher-data/conf/fwcw/conf/una/950905174345.txt

Francis E. Godwyll, Ph.D.
Ohio University, Athens, USA
2009

ACKNOWLEDGMENTS

MUCH OF THE MATERIALS IN this book are firsthand accounts resulting from working on the Trokosi emancipation and rehabilitation program for over a decade. The Trokosi story would have been different were it not for the intervention of the following people and organizations: International Needs Ghana and its Executive Director, Walter Pimpong, Mr. Mark Wisdom of Adidome who blew the whistle against the Trokosi system in the early 1980s, and Mr. U. S. Clarke, the District Secretary of North Tongu in the 1990s whose concern for women's rights led to the first governmental dialogue with Trokosi priests.

We wish to also acknowledge the efforts of Mama Adokuwa Asigble IV of Tefle and Togbui Komlaga Ribitim of Dorfor, two traditional rulers who distinguished themselves as champions for the change of an outmoded traditional practice. Our special appreciation goes to Justice Emile Short, Commissioner of the Ghana Human Rights and Administrative Justice Commission, who spent several years alongside the International Needs Ghana advocacy team to educate Trokosi practitioners and their communities. Thanks also go to the following University of Ghana Lecturers- Professor Elom Dovlo, Mr. Sosthenes Kufogbe and Professor Nukunya whose research and literary works greatly informed the writing of this book. We are grateful to Mito

Takeuchi, Ngan Nguyen, Christa Agiro, Elizabeth Ngumbi, and Bethany Debordes all graduate students of Ohio University for their assistance as well.

Last but not least we appreciate the opportunity Authorhouse Publishers has given us to make this work public. We believe that this story has to be told to a wider audience and by publishing the book they have made this possible.

CHAPTER 1

THE VOICES

INTRODUCTION

THE MAJORITY OF THE MEMBERS of civil society in the Republic of Ghana awoke to breaking news about the Trokosi with shock and disbelief. Ostensibly, apart from families of victims and some residents of the southeastern section of Ghana, this practice had persisted unknown to many. The tradition predominates among the Ewe and Dangme speaking peoples. But in the early 1990s the story of a 300-year-old tradition known in the Republic of Ghana in West Africa as Trokosi hit the airwaves and the print media. In this chapter, we will let the voices of two of the victims echo through these two narratives that capture their agonies in the Troxovi shrines.

THE VOICE OF YAWA MEWORLASE

The first voice to be heard is that of Yawa Meworlase, aged 38, a liberated Trokosi who served in the Avakpe shrine in the village of Avakpedome in the Volta Region of Ghana. Yawa originates from a village called Ahunda and has four children: Ernest Logodzo, 20 years; Rejoice Logodzo, 16 years; Belief Logodzo, 12 years; and Raymond Logodzo, 10 years. Yawa tells us: "I am the first born of 10 siblings. I was 8 years old and in primary school class three when I was taken to the Avakpe shrine."

JOURNEY TO THE SHRINE

One early morning, I was woken up and told to accompany my relatives to another town for a visit and I was very delighted. Little did I know it was to be a 'journey of no return.' The trip ended up in a village called Awakpedome where I was taken to a shrine, and some rituals were preformed for me. I was told that I had become a Trokosi. Although I was expected to stay permanently at the shrine from that day forward, the shrine priest made me to go back home with my relatives, because my parents could not pay for the entire fine they were asked to bring to the shrine (including me). Since it was a taboo as a Trokosi to attend school, I was withdrawn from school and stopped from any formal education. I cried each time saw my peers passing-by to and from school.

It took my relatives three years to save and procure all the required ritual items demanded by the shrine priest. On my return to the shrine, I was taken through the "amatsatsra" ritual where I was denuded, with only a strip of cloth between my thighs, and paraded through the community with a calabash on my head. My relatives carried my personal effects and took me to the shrine. After staying in the shrine with me for a few days, my relatives left but tricked me into believing that they were going back home and would be back in a few days. I cried for several days because the other inmates were strangers who spoke a different dialect from mine.

REASON FOR INCARCERATION

When I first asked why I was brought to the shrine, I was only told that it was to prevent my parents, siblings, and myself from dying. I got to know the real reason for my incarceration only recently and here is what I learnt. My aunt divorced her husband who did not appeal to her anymore. My aunt's husband was not pleased with the divorce and therefore pursued my aunt for the return of the bride price. My aunt sought refuge at the Avakpe shrine and collected 10 shillings and 3 pence from the priest to pay off her ex-husband. She thereafter continued to live with the priest in the shrine till she died. After her death, her siblings went to the shrine to demand her corpse for burial. Since my aunt was bonded to the shrine through the money she borrowed from the shrine priest, the demand for her corpse provoked the gods to wrath and a subsequent curse of death on my family. In order to lift the curse, the shrine demanded a replacement for her. I was therefore sent to atone for this "offense" I was given a new name at the shrine that is Mama.

SHRINE EXPERIENCE

During the first five days of my arrival at the shrine, all the beads and cloths were removed from my body and I was given "brissi" (navy-blue calico) to wear, with a "la" (woven raffia cord) around my neck. I was given a room to sleep in together with the other inmates. There were no doors, no window, no beds or sheets in the room. We spread mats on the floor without pillows to sleep on. On the second day of my stay in the shrine, I was given my daily responsibilities. I was to sweep the compound alone, fill all the pots with water, and wash all the dishes. I also had to carry all farm implements (hoes and machetes belonging to all Trokosi women who were incarcerated in the shrine before me) daily to and from the farm. Most of the time I worked on the priest's farm and carried the farm implements on an empty stomach.

Although I was just a child, I had to fend for myself by going to the bush to cut trees for firewood and burn charcoal for sale. I asked permission of the priest a number of times to go home for food when the situation was unbearable. Most times I couldn't go home because I had no money for transport.

When I was about 12 years, after my first menstruation, the priest requested to have sexual intercourse with me, but I was afraid and ran away. He threatened me several times. After my second menstruation he asked me one evening to get him something from his room. When I entered the room, he trapped me, pinned me down, and raped me. I had pains and was sore in my vagina. I ran away from the shrine and reported this to my parents. They consoled me and treated me with herbs. My mother was very angry but was afraid to complain for fear of the gods. After I felt better, I was sent back to the shrine.

I later realized that I was pregnant. I continued to work for the shrine priest on his farm until I was ready to deliver the baby. The priest sent me to my parents when I was due to deliver. My poor parents could not afford my hospital fee so they sought the assistance of a traditional birth attendant who delivered my baby boy. After three months' stay, my parents urged me to go back to the shrine. They always sent me back quickly to prevent fines by the priest, and or the wrath of the gods. I returned to the shrine to take care of the baby alone without any support from the priest. Life in the shrine continued to be harsh and full of hunger and all manner of deprivations until I had my fourth child. My children had no education, no medical care, and no nutritious food. I shared the same room and sleeping mat with them and my other colleagues in the shrine. My children helped me daily on the priest's farm.

LIBERATION

At the shrine, one day, Mr. Mark Wisdom came to the shrine to preach to us about salvation and freedom from enslavement. He said that God created us to be free and not to be slaves. Mr. Mark Wisdom was able to convince the shrine priest to allow us to learn dressmaking in the nearby town of Adidome. Mr. Mark Wisdom apprenticed us to a dressmaker until we were admitted to the International Needs Vocational Training Center (INVTC). Some of us went to INVTC but the priest got angry and stopped us. I, however, went back to learn dressmaking at INVTC after my liberation from the shrine, a skill which I still practice today.

Although rituals were performed by the shrine priest to set me free, my family members were still afraid of the power of the gods to punish them. Due to this fear, I was sent back to the shrine to perform widowhood rites when the shrine priest died. Now I am a Christian, baptized in our local Roman Catholic Church, in my community of Ahunda. I am very grateful to God for all that he has done for me.

RHETORICAL QUESTIONS:

Two questions that come to mind are:

* What is it that keeps the 'inmates' from fleeing even though there are no imposed physical barriers to cage them in?
* What made the relatives and parents capitulate in fear and refuse to respond to the suffering of their kin at the hands of the priest?

The Voice of Mercy Senahe

The second voice is that of Mercy Senahe, 27 years old, from Mafi-Aklamador, who was incarcerated in the Aklidokpo Shrine also at Avakpedome. There are two shrines in Avakpedome-the Avakpe, the older shrine, and the Aklidokpo, a more recent shrine. Mercy Senahe now resides in Adidome. She has three children: Faustie Logodzo, 13 years; Amegbe Logodzo, 10; and Mary Logodzo, 4 years.

I used to be called Mercy Togodo, but I have changed my surname to Senahe, which is simpler to pronounce. I was born at Yeji where my parents had migrated to do fishing along the Volta Lake. I was between eight or nine years old when I was brought from Yeji to Avakpedome, Togbe Aklidokpo's shrine. I was then in primary school, class three, living with my grandmother in another village.

Journey to the Shrine

My journey to the shrine started one day when my grandmother told me to accompany her to visit my parents at Yeji. When we got to Yeji I was told we had to travel further to our hometown at Aklamador for our annual festival. I was very excited. About a week later, we all arrived at Aklamador. We stayed there for about a month.

One early morning I was going to fetch water to have my bath when a young girl of about 10 years old informed me that she heard my parents whispering that I would be taken to a place of no return. I got frightened and ran away to our farm which was about a three hour walking distance. I hid myself in the bush on the farm till evening when I got hungry and afraid. I came out of the thicket where I hid myself and there stood my grandfather. He got very furious and rained insults on me. He cut a branch of tree and beat me along the bush path till we got home. Every one was angry with me in the house. Without taking my bath, I was

6

given a dress to wear and was dragged into a canoe where we crossed the Volta River to Adidome. We walked for over an hour from Adidome to Avakpedome that night.

We spent the night in the house of one of the sons of the priest of the shrine. The next day I was told to take my bath and was handed over to a "nudola," the woman responsible for dressing up a Trokosi for initiation. She dressed me up in beads on my ankle, knee, waist, wrists, arms, and neck. A red strip of "egoh" was folded with other cloths and passed in between my thighs, with the ends loosely sweeping the floor.

My mother and grandmother carried my personal items for use in the shrine. These included two half pieces of unsown cloths, two containers each of pomade and powder, comb, mat without pillow, a bucket, bowl, one bottle of perfume, two yards of calico, a hoe and a machete. And ¢60,000 (cedis) ($6.00) was added to the drinks for the priest.

On the way to the shrine, I was given a small calabash "akpe" which was placed on a big pad on my head to carry. Some cowry shells and colonial currencies (coins) were placed in it. There was a large crowd that followed us. Some of them stared, marveled, rejoiced, sang happily and said all kinds of things about me. People are always excited to follow the crowd to the shrine because it always yields them glasses of alcohol to drink, which they did.

REASON FOR INCARCERATION

I was told that one day, my maternal great-grandmother known as Omofoe Senahe, had a visitor in the evening. She played hostess to the strange woman who was later found to be a Trokosi. She was given food and a place to sleep till the next day. While leaving, she forgot her gold earrings in the room. My great-grandmother saw the earrings and kept them in a safe place. However, her sister, Ablakpoe Senahe, found the earrings, secretly took them, sold them, and used the money to travel to Yeji.

The stranger returned in search of her earrings. Realizing the embarrassment she found herself in, Omofoe denied seeing the earrings. The woman was grieved and so reported the offence at Avakpe and Korloe shrines at Avakpedome and Mafi-Dugame, respectively. She pronounced a curse of death upon the entire family of the one who stole her gold earrings.

Not long after the curse, the Senahe family members started dying mysteriously, one after the other, until the cause was traced to the lost earrings. Ablakpoe finally confessed the offense. One of my grandmother's daughters called Dzanu was required to submit her daughter, Adzo, who was sent to the Avakpe shrine, to appease the gods and intervene in the tragedy that had befallen the family.

It was later found again that members were still dying after the intervention. When soothsayers were consulted, it was revealed that another curse was pronounced at Korloe shrine. Ablakpoe's daughter, called Yedonya, now residing at Fodzoku, was also sent to Korloe shrine for the same crime. When Adzo died at the Avakpe shrine, I was sent to the Avakpe shrine as a replacement.

SHRINE EXPERIENCE

We went straight to "kpoganu," the central shrine where I was handed over to the priest amid libation and initiation rituals. My grandfather said, "This is your wife. We brought you someone previously but she died. We have brought you a replacement. This is the new person you have appointed." The priest responded, "I receive her."

The rest of the items were given to the priest. Some of the drinks were shared among the crowd and they rejoiced. We continued to the "kporvieme" the smaller shrine, the residential shrine for all Trokosis.

I was introduced to 21 other Trokosis who were serving in the shrine before me. There were four rooms in the hut without windows or doors. I was made to join five others in one of the rooms. We spread our mat bare on the floor and slept without pillows. I was made to sleep close to my predecessor, the last Trokosi who came before me. Before I left the shrine, six other girls were brought to serve as Trokosis.

Before I slept, my parents removed all the beads around my neck and waist, leaving a few on my waist and joints. Then I was handed over to the priest, who in turn handed me over to the oldest woman in the shrine; my parents left, promising to return the next day. But that was the end. I never saw them again. They left and I cried for days and weeks.

My father didn't go to the shrine with us. In fact he was unhappy with the whole issue. Since the crime originated from my maternal relatives, it meant I was a "borrowed" fellow from my paternal relatives because we are patrilineal. Thus, my maternal grandfather and grandmother, including my mother, sent me to stop their relatives from dying.

I soon found the reason for sleeping close to my predecessor. She woke me up about 4 a.m. and gave me orientation on my duties and responsibilities in the shrine, which started that dawn. She gave me the following instruction:

- As a new Trokosi you are taking over from me all the duties assigned to me when I came. You will do these and continue to pray for another Trokosi to be brought until she takes over from you. You should recite your prayer as you perform your duties daily.
- You must wake up at 4 a.m., sweep the whole compound, and fetch water to fill the priest's big pot in the shrine.
- You must run errands for everybody in the shrine.
- After sweeping, you must burn incense (dudzor dodo) using palm fruit waste every day, non-stop.

+ You must grind "eto" (a type of plant); adding a little water at a time till it turns red. Use this to smear all the idols in the shrine.

+ After household duties in the morning, collect the hoes and machetes of all the Trokosis in the shrine, and a pot of drinking water in a large pan, and carry them to the farm and back after work.

+ On "anyirogbe or agasigbe" (non-farming days) wake up very early and perform your duties. Grind "etoh" and polish the priest's idols and prepare to receive all the visitors to the shrine, who come for various purposes.

+ When you hear of the death of someone in town, wake up at dawn and burn palm branch incense everyday until the day the corpse has been buried.

+ Don't leave the shrine unless permission is granted to you by the priest to go home temporarily and collect food.

These instructions and other ones that followed were given to me as the days went by. I assumed my responsibilities right away. The compound was very big and I was given a broom to sweep it alone. I collected the rubbish and threw it away. I filled the pot with water, which I carried on my head in a bucket. While I was performing these duties, I recited the following:

+ *Adzo neva mia kplonu* (Adzo should come let's sweep)
+ *Abla neva mia kpalo nu* (Abla should come let's sweep)
+ *Aku neva mia kplo nu* (Aku should come let's sweep)

I recited these words using the different weekday names for females until the seventh day is mentioned, and the cycle is repeated. I continued to repeat this invitation rhyme until another Trokosi was brought to whom I also handed over my schedule.

After filling the pots that day, I ground "eto" and polished all the idols. It was frightening to touch these idols which represented the deities or gods in the shrine who had the ability to kill, punish, hear, see, watch over, protect, and so forth. The machetes and hoes of all my colleagues in the shrine were piled in a large bowl and set on my head to be carried to and from the farm. My parents left ¢200 ($ 0.20) with the old woman in the shrine. She gave me part to buy food before going to the farm. She gave me the money in bits until it got finished and I had to fend for myself.

FARMING

On the farm, the priest came around and gave equal portions of land to each person to till, no matter how old. It was very difficult for me at the beginning. I kept weeding and tilling the land until everybody left me. I was afraid to go to the shrine so I hid on the farm, but the priest found me, beat me and sent me back. Nobody was willing to assist her colleague because everyone has to quickly go and utilize the little time left before dusk to do some extra work in order to get food for herself and her children. The usual thing that brings some little income is to work for people on their farm for a small fee, or you cut trees to sell for firewood, or burn it into charcoal and sell it for money. We have to hide the money; often otherwise the priest takes it all from you.

My first day on the farm was tedious. My hands blistered but I still could not complete weeding my portion. The next day a fresh portion was added to the previous days, which I struggled to weed. I kept carrying forward my portion of plot for weeding until I learnt to weed a portion given me within a day.

When the ¢200 left for me was used, I engaged in cutting wood into firewood for sale. I learnt how to make charcoal which I sold. I learnt to be submissive and run errands for the older Trokosi women in the shrine and earned some food from them. I also weeded farms for people in exchange for my daily meals. Even though we worked on the farm for the priest daily we were denied access to the farm produce. He would not feed us even when we went and worked on his farm for a whole day.

Our relatives were supposed to take care of all our needs in the shrine but they forsook us. For all the 16 years I spent in the shrine it was only once that my mother visited me and no more. During harvest time, the priest and his relatives kept keen eyes on us so that we did not take any of the crops being harvested. Sometimes when our hunger became unbearable we would hide ourselves in the crops and uproot cassava or pluck corn which we roasted and ate. But we, had to dig holes and burry the corn husks and sticks of cassava to prevent detection. If caught eating the produce, you would be heavily sanctioned.

SANCTIONS

We were sanctioned for a number of acts considered misdemeanors against the priest or gods. These included eating farm produce, inability to complete weeding your assigned portion of land, attempting to run away from the shrine, breaking taboos, telling lies, refusing to have sex with the priest. Those attracted physical beatings by the priest, paying fines by the Trokosi herself or her relatives, tilling the land, subjection to forced sex and so forth.

The priest selects only one person among the Trokosis to cook for him, another took over only when she fell sick. He gave her money on market days. This money was often too small for food. That made the Trokosi to complain bitterly and resulted in quarrels between her and the priest. Almost invariably she ended up providing food from her own resources to feed the priest. The priest that I served was married before being installed as a priest. As a result of his installation as a Troxovi priest the wives left him because if they stayed as wives, their relatives would have to give Trokosis to the shrine after their death. The priest decided any time to have sex with any of us. Whenever he beckoned any Trokosi to his hut the only reason was to have sex with you and leave you to your fate when you got pregnant. Most of the time the women would refuse to heed his call. However, at night, while we had all gone to bed he would enter a room and begin to struggle with you for sex. He would beat you up if you resisted and rape you, while the others and our children looked on.

SEX AND CHILDCARE

When I turned 12 years old, I had my first menstruation. As a taboo I was sent to sleep alone in a small hut behind the shrine. At the end of my period the priest was informed and he performed "fla" cleansing ritual for me.

Two days later, while I lay beside my colleague Trokosi, the priest came in the night and jumped on me, pressing me hard to the bed. I struggled but he inserted his manhood inside me and raped me to his satisfaction. I started bleeding profusely and cried. My mates came and consoled me, urging me to be quiet because it happens to everybody in the shrine. The next day the blood continued to flow and the old woman gave me some herbs to treat the sore to stop the flow of blood.

From this first experience, I became pregnant and had to fend for myself. The priest only saw that my stomach was becoming big. There was no access to a hospital for medical care for pre-and post-natal care for a Trokosi in the shrine. When I was due to deliver, the priest sent me away from the shrine, without any money, to go to my parents. I borrowed money from a mate and left. I had a baby girl a week later. My father was still not very happy with my situation. My mother was content that I had a baby from the shrine, and she did everything possible to send me back since my presence in the house was likely to breed more deaths in the family.

Barely three months after giving birth, my parents sent me back to the shrine with only enough money to pay my debt and a little food to last for a few days. I named my child Awusi because I gave birth to her on a Sunday. The priest named her Dzatugbe which is a shrine name, and Gobu, the name of the priest's grandmother. I hate both names. My daughter is now called Faustie, a new name I have given her after leaving the shrine.

I assumed my normal duties in the shrine as soon as I returned. This continued for 1½ years when the priest repeated his act by raping me and sent me to my parents in Yeji to deliver the baby. For the third pregnancy, I decided to deliver in the shrine precinct, that is, where we reside during our menstruation. This is because the number of my children had increased and it became expensive to travel with all of them to and from Yeji. I returned to the shrine soon after each delivery.

LIBERATION

While at the shrine, I made some attempts to run away but I was always faced with the problem of where to go, how to go, and what to do. Most Trokosis would be welcomed by their mothers; however, my case was different. My grandfather pressured my mother to ensure that I was sent to the shrine, and she desperately pursued that to satisfy her family. My mother is a staunch traditionalist, very much afraid that the gods will kill her and her relatives who initiated the offense against the gods. My father converted to Christianity so he was against my being sent to the shrine.

After my first three years in the shrine, there was hunger in the whole community. I joined my mates to fetch palm kernel from incinerators to crack and chew. I decided to abscond from the shrine and go to my

14

mother. Some mates asked permission to go home for food and they never returned, so the priest was reluctant to grant me permission. I absconded to my mother and narrated my suffering, everybody cried. But after three months, my mother sent me back to the shrine. There were only two Trokosi women left when I retuned. Later, I run away again and went to issue a threat to my grandfather, the one who originally took me to the shrine. I threatened him that I was going to convert to Christianity. This frightened him so much that he went to seek permission for a temporary release for me. My grandfather had to pay the following for my temporary release: two sheep, two goats, one white cockerel, four bottles of imported Schnapps, four bottles of akpeteshie (local gin), ¢10,000 ($1.00), some money for a new "akpe" (calabash). After the "fla" cleansing rituals, I was given a temporary release.

I could have gone to my parents but knowing that I would be sent back again, I went to seek refuge at the International Needs Vocational Training Institute Center (INVTC) where I was given shelter, food, clothing, and toiletries. I had earlier attempted to visit this center with my colleagues to learn some skills, but the priest came with policemen to arrest us and sent us back to the shrine. This, however, became my last refuge where I stayed and learnt dressmaking for three years. I tried to visit my mother but she mistreated me so I came back to INVTC to learn bread baking and confectioneries which I now do for a living.

I am currently employed by INVTC as a kitchen staff and earn a salary to supplement my other income. INVTC has rented a place for me where I live with my children as a single parent. My children are enrolled in school through the assistance of INVTC which also pays for school uniforms and school fees.

Conclusion

It is worth noting that most Ghanaian children are given names based on the day they were born. Thus, by making reference to female names in her ritual songs, Mercy Senahe was in effect invoking malevolent spiritual forces to cause another Trokosi to be brought to the shrine so that she (Mercy) can hand over the daily shrine chores to the new Trokosi and be free. In other words, it should be seen as a prayer of distress. Whether the coming of another Trokosi to the shrine is a direct answer to this prayer or a mere coincidence, the fact that the cycle gets repeated each time a new inmate is added to the fold reinforces the belief in the efficacy of this "prayer of distress." The decision by the Trokosi priests not to care for the Trokosis and their children is a strategic one. The reason for this decision is to make sure that the Trokosis are fully occupied and focused on the challenge of finding their daily bread to the extent that they have no time to fellowship with other Trokosis and can not plan to execute any group revolt at the shrine.

These narratives are just two of the many stories of the victims and inmates of the several shrines dotted across the Volta region of Ghana. Even though the individual stories were different from each other, certain patterns emerged. In each case, there was a perceived wrongdoing that generated consequences. There was a community or family response to the ostensible wrong in order to avert the consequences. As a result, there was a concerted effort to ensure compliance to whatever prescriptions the priests gave. The victims were denied all rights of self-dignity, raped, and left uncared for even during pregnancy. Parents and relatives virtually abandoned their innocent children, lied to them, coerced them, and sometimes forced them back whenever they escaped. The victims feel helpless since nobody will stand up for them. To better understand the underpinning philosophy that made all these abuses possible, there is the need to dig deeper into the culture of the Ewes.

CHAPTER 2

GHANA AND THE

EWE ETHNIC GROUP

INTRODUCTION

THE REPUBLIC OF GHANA, NAMED after the medieval Ghana Empire of West Africa, lies 500 miles south of the old Ghana which was located between the Senegal and Niger rivers. This is the country that played host to the system from which the voices of agony from chapter one emanate. To give a context to the stories we will provide a historical background to both the country and the ethnic group (the Ewes) so that our readers who are unfamiliar with this land can build some meaningful associations.

THE PEOPLE OF GHANA

The people of present-day Ghana allude to strong connections with the medieval kingdom. For example, some inhabitants trace their ancestry to the old empire. Notable amongst these are the Mande and Voltaic people of Northern Ghana (the Mamprussi, the Dagomba, and the Gonja). Some anecdotal evidence also connects the Akan tribe to this great empire. The Akans cite semblances in names like Danso shared by the Akans of present-day Ghana and Mandikas of Senegal/Gambia, who had strong links with the empire. Gold mining is another occupation that links the new to the old. The empire was known for its caravans of gold and the new Ghana is said to have the second largest gold deposits in the world next to South Africa.

The map depicts the present-day Ghana boarded by Cote D'Ivoire, formerly Ivory Coast, to the west; Burkina Faso, formerly Upper Volta, to the north; Togo to the east, and the Atlantic Ocean (the Gulf of Guinea) to the south. Thus, Ghana, a former British colony, is an English speaking country, surrounded by French-speaking countries.

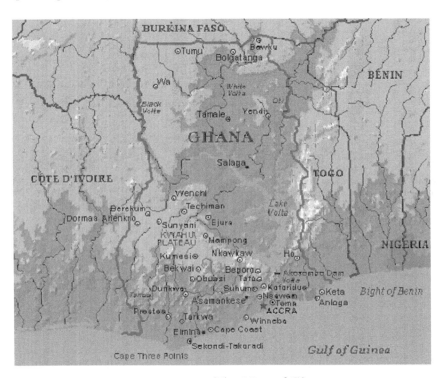

Figure 1. **The Map of Ghana**
Source: www.ghanaweb.com/imagelib/dest/12307026.gif

Present-day Ghana is located on West Africa's Gulf of Guinea only a few degrees north of the Equator. Half of the country lies less than 152 meters (500 ft.) above sea level, and the highest point is 883 meters (2,900 ft.). The 537-kilometer (334 miles) coastline is mostly a low, sandy shore backed by plains and shrubs and intersected by several rivers and streams, most of which are navigable only by canoe. A tropical rain forest belt, broken by heavily forested hills and many streams and rivers, extends northward from the shore, near the Cote d'Ivoire frontier (Ghana Home Page, 2009).

CLIMATE, LAND, FLORA AND FAUNA

Ghana has a tropical climate with seasons and elevation determining the variations in temperatures. Thus, it has wet and dry seasons. The wet or rainy period stretches from April to September in the north, whereas the south has a major rainy season from April to August and a minor season from September to November. The rainy season is influenced by the southwest monsoon winds blowing from the Atlantic Ocean, and the dry period is dominated by the northeasterly winds called the Harmattan, blowing from the Sahara desert, usually from December to March. The dry season lowers humidity, creating hot days and cool nights, especially in the north. The height of the Harmattan is experienced in the south in January.

Factors such as elevation and vegetation also influence the amount of rainfall, which varies from 1,100 mm (about 43 in) in the north to 2,100 mm (about 83 in) in the southeast. These factors, combined with location usually make the north hot and dry, the southwest corner hot and humid, and the eastern coastal belt warm and relatively dry.

Ghana is generally a lowland country, but the eastern border has a range of hills and a sandy coastline. In the west, the terrain is broken by heavily forested hills and many streams and rivers. The middle belt is the forest region and produces most of the country's cocoa, minerals, and timber. To the north lies an undulating savanna portion (grassland with scattered trees) that is drained by the Black and White Volta Rivers, which join to form the Volta, which then flows south to the sea through a narrow gap in the hills. The northern two-thirds of the country are covered by low bush, a park-like savanna, and grassy plains.

Much of the natural vegetation of Ghana has been destroyed by land cleared for agriculture; but trees such as the giant silk cotton, African mahogany, and cedar are still prevalent in the tropical forest zone of the south. Animal life has also been depleted, especially in the south; but it remains relatively diverse and includes leopard, hyena, buffalo, elephant, wild hog, antelope, and monkey. Many species of reptiles are found, including the cobra, python, puff adder, and horned adder.

One of the largest artificial lakes in Africa, the Volta Lake extends from the southeastern portion of Ghana to Yapei in the north (about 520 kilometers, or 325 miles). The lake is dammed at a town called Akosombo to provide hydroelectric power. The Akosombo hydroelectric plant is the major source of electricity for the country. The lake, however, provides inland transportation, fishing opportunities, and is a valuable potential for irrigation and farming.

The Trokosi system is prevalent in the ketu district of the southeastern part of the Volta region, as well as North and South Tongu districts among the Ewe-speaking ethnic group which constitutes about 12.7% of Ghana's population based on the 2000 census. This Ewe-speaking ethnic group stretches from this portion of Ghana to the southern half of Togo and to the southwestern portions of the Republic of Benin. Due to the arbitrary boundaries drawn during the colonial era, the Ewes now live in three distinct countries: Ghana, Togo, and Benin. The Trokosi system is however prevalent in all these three countries ostensibly due to common heritage. Boateng (2001) indicates that the Trokosi practice stretches to include some parts of Yoruba land in Nigeria.

Major Physical Features and Vegetation of the Volta Region

In terms of physical features and vegetation, the area has dry coastal plains to the south, which extend all the way to Benin. There are lagoons, streams, and small rivers, linked to the Volta River. There is a long stretch of sandbars bordering the Atlantic Ocean and the lagoons. The soil is not arable and land is scarce; the main occupation is therefore fishing. The northern portions have savanna vegetation with tall grasses, Baobabs, and small trees. The vegetation along the Volta banks is greener and richer. Even though fishing is an important mainstay among the Ewes, they are also trades as in farming, kente weaving, pottery, basket making, poultry farming, and carpentry.

The Structure of the Society and Belief Systems

According to Amenumey (1997), the Ewes of southeastern Ghana, like most groups in present-day Ghana, immigrated to their new home a few centuries ago. He argues that the Ewes migrated from Ketu in what is now the Republic of Benin, making a number of stops of varying durations on their way to their present settlement. Some historians have indicated that this point of departure happened around the time of the episode of the "Tower of Babel" known as the "Belebele" by the Ewes. Others have suggested the origins are from Mesopotamia, Egypt and so forth, but Amenumey concludes that there are no scientific bases for all these assertions. He places the arrival of the Ewes in their present home in the late 16th or early 17th century, which he says, recent archaeological analysis supports.

As it is among different ethnic groups in Ghana, the original founders of settlements became chiefs or formed the royal family out of which chiefs emerge. According to tradition, the type of chieftaincy institution that the Ewes adopted was the constitutional head and that became the basis of their political organization. Westermann (1935) supports this view. The Ewes are patrilineal, and ascendancy to the position of a chief is hereditary yet elective within the particular lineage or clan. Other viewpoints hold that some "royal families" trace their ancestry to the leaders in Ketu and Notsie before and during the migration to their present home (Amenumey, 1997).

It is important to understand that the social organization of the people is built around the clans and lineages. According to Nukunya (1997c), the clan is a "group of people who are believed to have descended patrilineally from a common putative ancestor and share the same totemic and other observances" (p. 48). He further states that even though membership is usually through birth, traditions show that in the past, masters incorporated strangers and slaves into their clans and accorded them full membership status. The definition of a clan as provided earlier does not apply to the "stranger clans," since even though recruitment is based on patriliny, the original composition was not necessarily made up of people with common patrilinealities.

According to Nukunya (1997c), Anlo lineage is "a branch of a clan found in a settlement which comprises all persons, male and female, who are able to trace relationships by series of genealogical steps through the male line to a known ancestor and theoretically to each other" (p. 50). Nukunya further explains that it is an exogamous group of nearly 10 generations, which is named after its founding ancestor and has as symbols of unity some of the following: an ancestral shrine, a stool, a leader and common property. Every member of the group is entitled to a number of rights and privileges including a plot of land to cultivate, a creek to fish in, a place to live, and a group to care for him or her in time of need—traditional social network. The following are some of the responsibilities of the head of the lineage:

- Administers the lineage land and other property
- Included in all transactions concerning lineage
- Judges disputes
- Represents lineage on the town's governing council
- Serves as chief ritual specialist
- Serves as a link between the living and the dead
- He is the only one with sufficient authority to officiate communication with the ancestors.

The lineage also becomes the fulcrum around which social control of the society revolves and the leader of the lineage is the "presiding officer." According to Abotchie (1997b), the head of the lineage serves as an administrative head, an acknowledged representative of the ancestors, a chief priest who performs religious sanctions deemed crucial to keep the lineage in beneficent relationship with the supernatural. Thus, with such an organizational structure the entire lineage is prone to follow the dictates of the head. So should the head inform them that for the lineage to avoid anger and punishment from the spirit world, they have to send one of their virgin daughters to pacify the gods or atone for a particular wrongdoing or sin, the whole lineage will more likely than not fall in line. This community level compliance is reinforced by their perception of social control which we will expound upon here.

The following beliefs underpin the Ewe society's perception of social control as alluded to by Abotchie (1997b). These, to a large extent, will explain some of the mental frames that support the Trokosi system.

- Ancestral spirits and other benevolent supernatural forces are believed to embody justice and fair play. The lineage head therefore presides over the traditional moral code. There is a strong belief that the ancestors maintain an active interest in the general welfare of society and will punish anyone who violates the traditional moral code. This belief gives both currency and potency to these norms or moral codes.

- The legitimacy of an individual's action is therefore judged against the traditional moral code. As the administrator who is also seen as the political head at the lineage level, it behooves the head to interpret the code to lineage members as well as enforce the sanctions attached to violations of the code.

- Sanctions exacted for crimes can be seen as both secular and sacred. In the sacred domain, the most extreme penalty is seen as expulsion from the lineage. The implications are devastating in the sense that it is a "loss of place and rights in the ancestral cult, the loss of protection by the ancestors both on earth and in the land of the dead and the loss of rights to incarnation" (Abotchie, 1997a, p. 74).

In the domain of secular sanctions, expulsion means the loss of economic, political, and social privileges deriving from lineage membership. Usually expulsions are invoked against serious transgressions such as homicide or incest. For lesser offenses the penalties may be the "loss of the right to land use, the imposition of fines or special duties, refusal to help in marriage payments, ostracism and a variety of other punitive measures considered commensurate with the gravity of offenses" (Abotchie, 1997a, p. 75).

- There is a prevalent belief in the collective responsibility of the whole lineage for crimes committed by any one member as stated earlier.

This collective responsibility notion is so compelling that it is seen as the traditional moral code. It compels individuals to have a say in the lives of other members of the clan in so far as their behavior deviates from the norm.

+ There is also a belief that the supernatural forces, for reasons best known to them, choose to spare the wrongdoer and instead strike an innocent member of the lineage. This may be one of the major motivators of the lineage head, as well as all members, to act individually and collectively in accordance with the moral code.

+ This unsettling belief particularly keeps lineage members uncomfortable when one kin strays. Thus the lineage does all that is in its power to bring recalcitrant kin to compliance.

Abotchie notes that the efficacy or failure of the private control mechanism of the lineage depends on the effective redemption of the secular and sacred obligations of the lineage for which the lineage head is ultimately accountable to the supernatural forces, since he is personally also subject to their judgment. Thus ultimately the final authority resides in the supernatural forces who thus become the final arbiters of social action, since whatever is ultimately done must be sanctioned by these forces (1997b, p. 76).

Traditionally, Ewes believe in corporal punishment, and the clan has to carry it out or it becomes the object of vengeance. In a situation where a culprit evades punishment by fleeing, his or her clan suffers the penalty. In the same vein, the offended party is entitled to help from the clan. Nukunya (1997b) supports this view. The Ewe word for vengeance, "hlorbiabia" literally means "asking the clan." In other words, in everyday parlance, the price to pay for a crime is exacted on the clan or the clan stands in debt to pay for the actions of the offender. The Trokosi system is a typical example of the belief in corporal punishment by Ewes.

CONCLUSION

It is clear from the description of the societal structure of the Ewes that the pillars critical to establish a system feared and dreaded by the people is already in place. It is therefore no wonder that individual interest and liberties become submerged in the interest of the larger society. As we delve into the Trokosi system in the next chapter, the correlations between the organization of the society as a unit and the belief in the Trokosi system will become even clearer.

CHAPTER 3

THE TROKOSI SYSTEM

INTRODUCTION

WHY SHOULD THE "FATHERS EAT sour grapes and the children's teeth be set on edge?" (Ezekiel 18:2; Jeremiah 31:29). Apparently in the southeastern part of Ghana where the Trokosi system is practiced, this is a worthwhile question to ask. It is also the case that the biblical proverb partially quoted above exemplifies exactly what happened in the Trokosi practice.

DEFINITION/MEANING

Trokosi is a combination of two Ewe words "tro" and "kosi." The word "tro" means god or deity and "kosi" means slave. Trokosi therefore means "slave of deity." Trokosi is a traditional system whereby, virgin girls as young as six years of age are sent into Troxovi shrines as reparation for wrongs purported to be committed by a family member. It is worth noting that although the Ewes have several deities that they worship, it is only Troxovi shrines (i.e., deities that receive children) that practice

27

the Trokosi system. The Trokosi system is founded on the belief in the supernatural power of the Troxovi (the gods) to search for wrongdoers and punish them. When an aggrieved person goes to the Troxovi shrine or mentions the name of a Troxovi to place a curse on a wrongdoer, it is believed that the Troxovi supernaturally searches for the wrongdoer and punishes the person by causing calamities and mysterious deaths in the wrongdoers' family. These calamities are believed to take several forms, such as strange sicknesses, incurable diseases, and unexplained occurrences, including deaths of family members. This confirms the belief in the collective responsibility of the whole clan for crimes committed by any one member (Abotchie, 1997a).

Possible Origins

A story narrated by Togbui Addo IV of Klikor in the Volta Region of Ghana tells about the possible origins of the Trokosi system. He narrated a mysterious event that happened in Benin resulting in a young virgin being brought to one of the shrines in Klikor. He said one day a household in Benin woke up to realize that everyone in the house had smoke oozing from the top of their heads. The family called on an elder who was also a Catholic priest to offer prayers. However, the strange phenomenon continued regardless of the prayers of the priest. The family then consulted a diviner who told them that someone in the family committed a crime and was cursed at a Troxovi shrine in Klikor. In order to avert the mysterious event, a young virgin girl had to be sent to the Klikor shrine. Togbui Addo went on to say that after the girl was brought and rituals performed at the Klikor shrine, the strange happenings ceased. Such occurrences give credence to the belief in the potency of virgins atoning for calamities.

The origins of the Trokosi system stretch back to antiquity and cannot be completely unraveled as one is dependent on oral tradition with its numerous handicaps. Some date the practice to the 17th century (Gadzekpo, 1993). Traditionally, it is claimed that Troxovi were brought from the original home of the Tongu people. The origins of the people of Tongu are traced to some parts of present day Nigeria. Oral tradition holds that it was the supernatural powers of these gods that guided them as they migrated to their present home (Dovlo & Adzoyi, 1995).

With regards to the geographic spread and prevalence of the practice of the Trokosi in Ghana, it is found among the Ewe and Dangme-speaking peoples of the southeastern coast of the country. On a wider scale, the practice is prevalent among the Ewe and Fon-speaking peoples along the west coast of Africa in Togo and Benin (Dovlo & Adzoyi, 1995). It is worthy of note that Dangme-speaking peoples call the practice Woryokwe, which also means slaves of deity. Thus, there is a consistency in the meaning of the word irrespective of which ethnic group practices it.

Sowah (1993), however, is of the opinion that the origins of some of the deities may not be that remote and ancient. He opines that Avakpe (the Troxovi of Avakpedome) may be associated with a hillock near the town of Avakpedome in the North Tongu District where the Avakpe shrine is located. The hillock is also known as Avakpe. Etymologically, the word Avakpe means "War" (Ava) "rock" (Kpe) (p. 82).

Some of the shrines in Ghana, such as Koklofu and Nyigbla, trace their origins to present-day Benin as the source of these shrines. Not only is the historical connection based on oral tradition, but there are also links existing currently between the people who own these deities and their Benin homes. This view is supported by the history of the Ewes, who were said to have migrated from Notsie in Dahomey, during the tyrannical rule of King Agorkorli of Notsie, to their present abode.

From interviews conducted by the authors, there is unanimity among Trokosi priests that Trokosi deities were originally war gods who helped the Ewe and Dangme-speaking people win wars during their migration in ancient times. Dovlo and Adzoyi (1995) confirm this view, stating:

> There is strong evidence that the Troxovi originally served as war gods. They are linked with the hazardous confrontations of migration and pre-colonial skirmishes with neighbors after settlement in their present homes. These gods are credited with the success of the Tongu in war. (p. 4)

However, Trokosi deities were used as policing agents during peacetimes to punish and deter wrongdoers.

ORGANIZATION

A typical Trokosi shrine consists of a number of huts clustered together and fenced around with palm branches. One of the huts houses the deity and ritual regalia. The priest occupies one of the huts and the Trokosi women and children live in the rest of the huts. A critical examination of the Trokosi system indicates that it hinges on the social organizational structure of the Ewes through clan organization as explained earlier. Specifically, a clan or family normally owns Troxovi shrines. The clan therefore installs priests to administer Trokosi shrines. Like any hierarchical command organizational structure, the clan or family elders, who are mostly males, serve as board of directors of the shrine. The priest administers the day-to-day affairs of the shrine and performs the rituals. An appointed female, called "zeklor" (one who washes the pots), assists the priest. The duty of the zeklor includes helping new Trokosi girls undergo rituals and adjust to shrine life. There is also a male assistant to the priest called the "ngorgbea" (front man). The main duty of the ngorgbea is to lead in ritual performance and to act as a linguist for the shrine. In shrines where the priest has died, the zeklor and ngorgbea act until the installation of a new priest.

Features/Characteristics

One of the key features of the Trokosi system is that wrongdoers receive their punishment indirectly through their relatives. It is believed that wrongdoers are the last to be punished after all family members have been exterminated by the Troxovi when steps are not taken to seek atonement at the Troxovi shrine. This feature of the Trokosi system reinforces the belief among the Ewe in corporate punishment. The belief is reinforced by sayings such as "deku deka gblea bubu awo" (one bad nut spoils the rest). This traditional belief in corporate punishment also resonates with Mosaic teachings of Yahweh visiting the sins of the fathers upon the children even unto the third and fourth generation (Deuteronomy, 5:9; Exodus, 20:5; Exodus 34:7; Numbers 14:18).

The offenses for which virgin girls are incarcerated in Troxovi shrines range from very trivial issues, such as using abusive language or stealing a tuber of cassava, to more grievous matters such as murder. In fact, it does not matter what type of wrong one commits. The issue rests more on the aggrieved person seeking vengeance by calling on a Troxovi name to pronounce a curse on the wrongdoer. When committed to the shrine, the Trokosi girl serves arbitrary sentences, ranging from a minimum of three years to lifelong servitude. It is also our observation that it is uncommon to find a Trokosi girl who has served a short period of time in the shrine and then been released.

In its most common and humiliating form, a virgin who is yet to experience menarche is given to a deity to atone for the sin or offense committed by a relative. She thus becomes a slave of the deity, although euphemistically she is called the deity's wife. She remains in the shrine serving the priest and other functionaries of the deity for a period ranging from a few years to life and is often used as the sexual partner of the priest (Nukunya & Kwafo, 1999b).

As slaves, the Trokosi women and their children are reduced to beasts of burden by becoming tillers of the ground, hewers of wood, and drawers of water. Another dehumanizing aspect of the practice is that the reparation is perpetual. What that means is that, whenever a woman sent into servitude dies, she is replaced by another young virgin. This aspect of the practice ensures continuity of the Trokosi system and provides a perpetual source of young girls to populate the shrines.

Children of Trokosi slaves suffer the same fate as their Trokosi mothers. Shrine priests neglect their children born with Trokosi slaves and the children are denied their basic rights and freedoms. Paramount among the rights is the denial of the right to education. Although basic education is free and compulsory in Ghana, Trokosi children are denied access to education because by a twist of fate, they happen to be born to Trokosi mothers and live in Trokosi shrines. Trokosi children are denied paternal care and grow up lacking a sense of identity and security.

The following two narratives typify the lives of ritual slaves. The first is the story of Dora Galley, a 22 year-old woman, who resided at Ative Minawoekope with her parents and six siblings. She was incarcerated for seven years at a shrine.

REASON FOR INCARCERATION

The reason for being a Trokosi is that my uncle had a sexual affair with a Trokosi. This resulted in deaths in my family. I was sent to the shrine to atone for the offense of my uncle. As a Trokosi, I was forced to have sex with the priest as one of the rituals in the shrine. My luck was that I did not get pregnant before we were liberated three and a half years ago.

I was also compelled to work on the farm of the priest from morning till evening without any payment or food from the priest. I had to cut down trees and uproot tree stumps to burn into charcoal to sell and make some money to take care of myself. As a Trokosi I did not have any right to take any crops from the farm unless the priest allowed me to. As a result of the meanness of the priest, I faced a lot of deprivation and hunger for most of the time. Occasionally my parents sent me some food stuffs but that was kept in the priest's room and I had to request it anytime I needed some.

I missed my parents and siblings, also my friends, very much when I was in the shrine. I could not leave the shrine to visit them because of the fear that a relative would die if I left the shrine. My relatives stopped visiting me in the shrine because they were worried about my constant crying anytime they visited me in the shrine. They were afraid that I would follow them home.

My parents were of great help to me initially, but they abandoned me. Some other Trokosi women helped me. I believed in the gods of the shrine since that was what I was introduced to. However, with the passage of time and the hardships I went through in the shrine, I started praying to the almighty God, for deliverance. As I prayed I became hopeful that something would happen one day for me to be free, and it did happen. I had the hope that something would happen.

For me International Needs Ghana is an organization concerned with fighting for the freedom of Trokosi girls and seeking to relieve them and other people from their pains. If it were not for the work of International Needs, I would have still been in bondage. I want to thank them very much for liberating us and giving us a vocation. Because of International Needs, I can now look forward to a fulfilling future.

I look forward to be equipped with tools to work with. I also wish that the fight to liberate the rest of those who are still in servitude in the

Trokosi shrines would go on. My wish is that, I will succeed in my chosen vocation and live an independent life. I was at the International Needs Vocational Training Center for three years and studied hairdressing after my liberation and rehabilitation where I learnt hairdressing.

After her liberation and rehabilitation, Dora had this to say:

> I personally dislike the Trokosi practice. I think that it is an affront to the dignity of women and is a practice that takes advantage of the meekness of women. How can someone else commit a crime and a young innocent girl goes to suffer in the shrine?

In other words why have the fathers eaten sour grapes and set the children's teeth on edge? It was an uncle of hers who had sex with a Trokosi. Why should Dora be made to pay for it when she had no part in the entire episode?

The second narrative is for Patience Akpoe, a 31-year-old female who hails from Mafi Kpogadzi. Patience spent 12 years at the shrine. Now after her liberation, she lives with her father Asidigbe Adzamade, and her mother, Asiehi Adzamade, at Yeji, a fishing town along the Volta River.

REASON FOR INCARCERATION

The reason for Patience's incarceration was that her uncle had sex with a Trokosi. Trokosis are supposed to be wives of the gods, and any man who has sex with them commits an offense against the gods and is punished. Her uncle drowned mysteriously and the family consulted soothsayers who told them to atone at the shrine for the offense. Here are the words of Patience telling about her ordeal, liberation, rehabilitation, future aspirations, and denouncement of the Trokosi system:

My experience in the shrine was a pathetic one in that I was reduced to a farm laborer and did other menial work. My family promised to send me food while I was in the shrine but abandoned me. To take care of myself I had to cut down trees to burn charcoal to sell before I could buy food to eat. My difficulties in the shrine included getting food to eat regularly, clothing, working on the farm for long hours, far beyond reasonable time, and being used as beast of burden to carry farm produce and to fetch water from the river for the priest.

I felt very bitter towards the priest - Torgbe Korleshie - when he impregnated me at the age of 16. The priest did not allow me to visit the clinic for prenatal care or go to the hospital. Throughout the pregnancy, I had to fend for myself.

I missed my family since I was only 10 years of age when I was sent there, even though they abandoned me to my fate. I very much longed for parental affection, which the shrine never provided. My best friend was called Shimekor. She was of great help to me. We shared together the little food we could lay hands on.

I believed in the worship of the Korloe god (the name of the god of the Korloe shrine). Among ourselves, we encouraged each other in the hope that one day we would be free. I did not know that I would indeed be liberated the way it happened. But it did happen through the work of International Needs.

I would like my child to be sponsored to the highest level of education. I wish for myself a joyous occasion and to go home with my tools to start my work together, with the funds that will be added. I spent 18 months at the International Needs Vocational Training Center and learnt hairdressing.

The most important thing in my life is my health, my job that I will be starting soon, and the education of my child. Above all, I am eager to vehemently protect the independence I am now enjoying. My future plans are to set up a hair salon to help take care of myself and my child, educate my child, and to be married to a responsible man.

International Needs means a lot to me. They gave me my freedom and my training. When they liberated others and me, they provided us with seed money to start life as independent people. I can now boast of having my own vocation to fend for my child and myself. I would encourage all to support the work of International Needs.

The practice of Trokosi is a crime and it should be stopped completely. Human beings are not animals to be sacrificed for flimsy issues such as sexual misconduct and theft. The government should move quickly to arrest and jail those who are still perpetuating this evil and dehumanizing practice by keeping and abusing young innocent girls in the shrines.

Trokosi Children

Interviews conducted with some priests, clearly show that those who were married and had children before becoming Trokosi priests have closer affinity with these children than the children born to them by Trokosi women. Most Trokosi priests consider intercourse with the Trokosi women as fulfilling a spiritual obligation to the gods because they see themselves as the physical representatives of the gods when they are ordained into the priesthood. The Trokosi women on the other hand are considered the wives of the gods. Trokosi children therefore are regarded as the children of the gods and not the children of the priest's although the priest's biologically fathered them. In accordance with this notion Trokosi children are given shrine names and do not bear the name of their biological father the priests. As part of the identity definition of their new role and status, Trokosi priests also stop using their given names and start using shrine names when they are ordained. As part of the package of punishment, any child born by a Trokosi is the responsibility of that Trokosi and her family, not the responsibility of the priest. It is therefore not uncommon to find priests who had children before becoming priests providing for those children and educating them to the highest level and neglecting children born to them by Trokosi women.

Why the System Thrives

Although a law was passed in 1998 by the government of Ghana criminalizing ritual servitude, the Trokosi practice still persists due to lack of enforcement of the law by responsible government institutions. Second, Trokosi-practicing communities still strongly believe and fear that the gods will cause mysterious deaths and calamities in their families if they stop sending their virgin daughters to the shrines as reparation for the sins of their forefathers. Third, there exist a group of traditionalists called the Afrikania Mission, who strongly believe that Trokosi is part of the cultural heritage of the people and therefore vehemently oppose every attempt to stop it.

Soothsayers play a vital role in sustaining the Trokosi system. The role of soothsayers came to the fore in an interview with Mr. Tsatsu Badagbor, a North Tongu District Assembly member from Mepe in the Volta Region of Ghana. He indicated that the role of soothsayers must be tackled because leaving them out of the equation would create a gap. Mr. Badagbor asserted that soothsayers are the ones who first divine and tell inquiring family members what is wrong with them and actually prescribe the object of reparation, invariably a virgin girl. He explained that there are numerous soothsayers and he thinks that they operate in a league. Furthermore, he said that once the first soothsayer divines and comes out with a prescription, other soothsayers will give the same outcome no matter how many more soothsayers are consulted.

The practice of Trokosi/Fiashidi/Woryokwe is closely linked to the Ewes and their close neighbors, the Dangmes and Krobos (Dovlo & Kufogbe, 1997), who have a common migration history. The people of Anlo refer to the system of Trokosi as Fiashidi, and the Dangmes and Krobos call it Woryokwe. The origins of the deities that receive women in bondage are traced to the Volta Region and beyond to the Republics of Togo and Benin (Dovlo & Kufogbe, 1997). Prior to the abolition of the practice at the Dadapiem of Big Ada, the Chief of Dangbebiawe had to travel all the way to Benin to inquire about the acceptability of change to the gods and the means of bringing about ritual abolition of the practice.

It is believed that since the gods who receive women as Trokosis are major gods of ethnic communities and clans, they cannot be fully operational outside their traditional geographical location. There are several reasons supporting this viewpoint.

First, most of these gods were acquired originally as war gods to serve these communities. It would be difficult to establish the shrines of such war gods in territories considered enemy territory in the past. Second, cultural practices relating to land ownership and tenancy militates against the spread of these shrines. Normally, shrines of the major gods of other ethnic groups are not allowed in other ethnic areas. The fear is that since these are ancestral gods, the physical presence of shrines to them can be used by people of associated ethnic groups to lay claims to land and other landed property in the future. In the Afram Plains District (North Kwahu District) of the Eastern Region, for instance, where a lot of Ewe-speaking people can be found, tenancy agreements do not permit tenants to establish such shrines. It was discovered that in the Afram Plains the chiefs did not only disallow such shrines but any one seeking the services of such shrines in the Volta Region had to first inform the chief (Dovlo & Kufogbe, 1997).

Third, one major role played by these shrines, which would have enabled their adoption in other areas of southern Ghana, is the role of supernatural adjudicator of cases (Dovlo & Kufogbe, 1997). Somehow this role was fulfilled in the other areas of southern Ghana, which are mainly Akan speaking, through their river deities - a famous one being the "Antoa Nyame." Earlier in the century improvement in communications opened the door to the more versatile medicine-drinking shrines of the Northern Region such as Tigare and Nana Tongo, etc. The spread of these, which was also known as anti-witchcraft shrines, may have preempted the spread of the Troxovi shrines (Dovlo & Kufogbe, 1997).

The Troxovi shrines may also have no attraction to the Akan because the practice is centered on women and the Akan is a matrilineal society. As Boateng (1995) argues, in a patrilineal society not much premium is put on the female segment of the society, consequently the lack of concern regarding the plight of the Trokosis (p. 32). Thus, the matrilineal system of the Akan may have forestalled the development or transplanting of such cults among them.

A fourth reason for the geographic limitation of the practice is offered by a priest, Torgbui Ahogbato of the Kaja shrine of Pokuase. According to Dovlo and Kufogbe (1997) the priest noted that the Troxovi deity does not travel far. It is believed that the farther it goes, the weaker its potency becomes. Thus the Trokosi practice, according to the authors, behaves according to a distance decay postulate in which the power of the gods to strike victims decreases with distance away from the home localities of the parent shrines (Dovlo & Kufogbe, 1998). Those shrines whose practices come close to the phenomenon are related to parent shrines in their home localities of origin but do not have the mandate of the parent shrines to carry out full Trokosi operations. Therefore, at best, they are operated as recruitment or satellite centers for subjects outside the active range or sphere of influence of the principal shrine and parent god. Such views about the diminishing power of the gods suggest that the female ritual bondage phenomenon might operate according to a distance decay postulate of geographical interaction where the core or center of energy radiation is the parent shrine, so the satellite or recruitment center/shrines constitute the periphery of decreasing the spatial interaction (Dovlo & Kufogbe, 1998). This according to them explains why Trokosi cannot be found in other parts of Ghana apart from the Volta, Greater Accra and the Eastern Regions. The shrines are not, however, without influence in areas outside the regions of dominance. Clients could come from anywhere in the world for atonement from far and wide, across the country, and the eastern borders from Togo and Benin, depending on their fame.

According to Nukunya and Kwafo (1999b), there were at least 39 Trokosi shrines in the southern Volta Region and the two Dangme districts of the Greater Accra region. In the North Tongu District, there were 18 shrines while in the South Tongu Districts there were 8 and 5 in the Ketu District. While there were 3 in the Keta District, in the Akatsi District, the Dzoli shrine at Avenorpeme (Suife) was the only Troxovi shrine, and in the Dangme East District, there were 2 whilst the Dangme West District had 3 shrines.

Clients come from far and near, although quite a large concentration of clients come from the Tongu area itself. According to the Tongu priests, the principal order of numerical importance is Tongu, Avenor, Anlo, some, northern Eweland (Ho, Hohoe, and Kpandu Districts), and Ada, Dzodze, Togo, Krobo and Kwahu areas. The network of clients is quite wide, extending far beyond the borders of Tongu, Eweland, and even Ghana (Nukunya & Kwafo, 1999b).

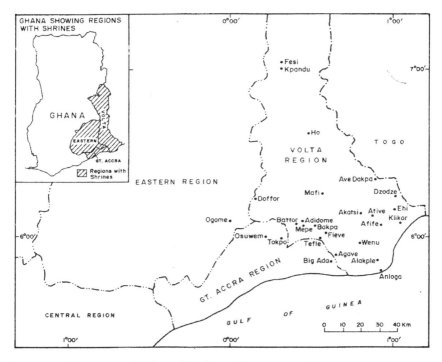

Figure 2. Location of Major Trokosi Shrines in Ghana
Source: (Dovlo & Kufogbe, 1997) Baseline Survey on Female Ritual "Bondage" in Ghana: The Geographical Spread and Count of Victims. A Report Prepared for ING and CIDA.

It is assumed that there are two types of Trokosis, those in confinement and those out of confinement. In some shrines at Klikor, for example, victims are released to their parents/guardians until puberty when they are re-confined (Dovlo & Kufogbe, 1997). Some remain in confinement until they marry. Confinement may take place at the outer precincts of the shrine. Victims may also be confined to an area surrounding the shrine or to a specific community. Victims living out of confinement are not totally free but come back to perform rituals on special occasions. When a victim dies, the family must replace her but, according to Dovlo and Kufogbe (1998), the large numbers of victims who do not live on the premises of the shrines present a problem in conducting a census of victims.

THE ROLE OF FEAR IN PERPETUATING THE TROKOSI SYSTEM

Mazrui , Ajayi, Boahen, and Tshibangu (1993) observed that:

> Religion impregnates the entire texture of individual and commercial life in Africa. The African is profoundly, incurably a believer, a religious person; religion is not just a set of beliefs but a way of life, the basis of culture, identity and moral values. Religion is an essential part of the tradition that helps to promote both social stability and creative innovation. (p. 501)

To a large extent the reason for the silence of many politicians over the Trokosi practice could be found in the words of Mazrui et al. (1993) Trokosi is not just a set of beliefs but a way of life, the basis of culture, identity and moral values of the Ewe people of the southeastern section of the Volta Region of Ghana. The Trokosi system as a traditional religious practice instills fear both in the ordinary citizen and the politician. The belief in the ability of the Troxovi deity and shrine to inflict pain and death on even people of other religious persuasions is very strong, hence the silence of politicians and law enforcement agencies or their inability to deal with it.

For example, the Mayor of Adidome, Mr. Sylvester Clarke the first government official to take on the task of ending the suffering of innocent girls, women and their children enslaved in the Trokosi practice did so because he was not an indigene of the area that practiced Trokosi. He therefore did not have the entrenched fear that local politicians had. Mr. Clarke had to approach civil society organizations for help because the District administration of which he was the head did not have the finances and human capital to deal with the enormity of the Trokosi issue. District Assemblies and administrations in Ghana are funded directly by the central government. Funds disbursed by central government to Districts are mostly designated for specific development projects such as building of schools, health care centers, and roads, provision of portable water and dealing with issues of sanitation. Hardly will central government make budgetary allocation for solving issues like Trokosi because it is localized and does not have a national character enough to merit the limited resources at the disposal of the central government. The paradigm in developing countries is that social issues such as Trokosi falls within the purview of civil society organizations and these organizations are better equipped and resourced to handle them.

CONCLUSION

In no uncertain terms the Trokosis serve the priests as slaves, who serve the gods of the shrines. They are used as beasts of burden to provide for the upkeep of the priests, exploited sexually, yet receive no normal human affection and denied of the simplest needs of life. These words contained in a report on the website of Every Child Ministries will serve as a fitting conclusion of this chapter.

They are said to be "wives" of the gods, although one must observe that these gods certainly do not treat their "wives" with any affection, respect or even human decency. This is a dehumanizing form of ritual abuse. These child slaves (Trokosis) are forced to chant praises to the idol gods, offer sacrifices and do heavy manual labor in the priest's fields all day without any compensation, while strictly forbidden to eat even a morsel of the grain they raise. Most Trokosi slaves live with constant hunger, and some of them are refused food. In such cases they have no alternative but begging or scrounging in garbage discarded by others (Every Child Ministries, n.d.).

CHAPTER 4

THE JOURNEY TO LIBERATION

INTRODUCTION

THE INSTITUTION OF TROKOSI HAS given rise to several problems. Most of these relate to the human rights abuse that the girls are subjected to and the place of obsolete customs in the modern state. In 1919, the work of individuals and various organizations exposed the practice to the then colonial administration, which caused some ripples, but the exposure in the 1980s was greeted with great indignation and outcry for action to stop the practice.

EARLIER PROTESTORS

Archival recordings in Ghana indicate that the first time the Trokosi issue came to the attention of the secretary for native affairs was in 1919 when Mr. Nyagbledzi a native of Battor in the North Tongu District complained to the colonial administration about the Trokosi practice. As a result of Nyagbledzi's complaint, the practice in Battor was banned in 1920. The ban was, however, lifted in 1924 after the Trokosi priest and chief of Battor petitioned the colonial administration. The report of the police commissioner of the Eastern Province exonerated the Trokosi practitioners. In his report, the police commissioner indicated that he found no law prohibiting the procedure. The report went on to attack Mr. Nyagbledzi and questioned his motives for writing to complain against the Trokosi practice. He was described as writing to show off, or seeing himself as the only fish in the river, because he was one of the few people in Battor who could read and write (National Archives of Ghana ADM.11/568, ADM.11/768).

Miers and Klein (1999), who reviewed the relevant literature on the issue of slavery and other forms of servitude and bondage during the colonial period, confirm the reluctance of colonial regimes to deal with issues related to slavery. The reluctance stemmed from the colonial administration's dependence upon such slavery practices to sustain the colonial economy and on slaveholding elites to administer the colonial empire.

One would have thought that the influence of the missionaries on the colonial administration would have made a difference in the attitude of the colonial office to this practice. But there was a very thin line between the missionaries and the colonial administration. Some see the missionaries as collaborators; others see them as forerunners for political domination. In other words, the missionaries came to soften the hearts of the people of the colonized world in order to allow the colonial authority to take over (Reagan, 1999).

The fact that some of the castles built along the coast of Ghana, which later became the transit quarters for slaves, had a church directly above the auction halls where human beings were sold may reflect the symbiotic relationship existing between the two groups. Even though slavery was technically supposed to have ended by the time of colonization, the fact that the missionaries and the state had such a close collaboration in the past cannot be overlooked, and this may also, to a large extent, explain the apparent silence of the colonial administration concerning this hideous and inhumane practice.

The Trokosi issue was revived in the late 1980s by Mark Wisdom, a native of Adidome and a French scholar who was born and bred outside the Tongu region. According to Mark Wisdom, he had a dream in Togo, where he was teaching at the time. In his dream he saw a giant who had imprisoned several women and there was no one to wrestle the keys of the prison from the giant to set the women free. However, he was able to take the keys of the prison from the giant to set the women free. Although he did not understand the dream at the time, he kept it in his memory knowing that he had a divine mission to fulfill.

Several years later when he visited his hometown of Adidome, he remembered the dream he had had earlier in Togo and made the connection to the Trokosi system. Mark Wisdom then called on the Trokosi priests to set the ritual slaves free. He wrote series of letters to the government at the time lamenting the plight of the girls. He also sought audience with the various traditional rulers in Tongu to add their voice to his advocacy work. His efforts resulted in a grand durbar in late 1986 where all the priests were summoned by the traditional rulers to a meeting to declare the system abolished. However, at the meeting the priests requested a postponement so that they could adequately prepare for the ceremony. To the chagrin of everyone, the priests refused to honor subsequent meetings.

Mark Wisdom later formed a non-governmental organization in late 1990s called the Fetish Slaves Liberation Movement to continue with his campaign, having worked with International Needs Ghana for some time. Other organizations such as Missions International and Sentinel of Switzerland, contributed in diverse ways to the struggle for the emancipation of the slaves. However, this chapter will focus more on the activities of the most dominant organization- International Needs Ghana - that championed the cause of Trokosi liberation.

In September of 1989, the then North Tongu District Secretary (Mayor) Sylvester Clarke visited the International Needs Ghana (ING) offices to request the intervention of ING in the Trokosi ritual servitude issue. In presenting the rationale for the intervention, Clarke recounted how he discovered hundreds of young virgin girls incarcerated in fetish shrines all over the Tongu region for crimes allegedly committed by relatives. The district secretary intimated that the girls suffered all forms of abuse, including rape, torture, forced labor, and hunger. In summary, the state of the Trokosi girls could best be described as deplorable.

In discussing the areas of intervention, the following were highlighted:

+ Human Rights Advocacy and Education on the Trokosi issue
+ Vocational skills training program for the Trokosi slave girls
+ Negotiation with fetish shrine priests and elders
+ Organizing emancipation ceremonies for Trokosi women
+ Provision of psychosocial, emotional, and vocational counseling for emancipated Trokosi women
+ Provision of other rehabilitation packages for liberated women, including housing needs, seed capital, and addressing the educational needs of Trokosi children
+ Provision of micro finance
+ Community follow-up counseling program. (Personal Communication Clarke, 2005)

In the early part of 1990, the North Tongu District Assembly organized a durbar of chiefs, queen mothers, Trokosi shrine priests, and elders to deliberate on the Trokosi problem. At that first meeting, all the seven paramount chiefs of North Tongu were of unanimous consensus that the Trokosi practice dehumanized the girls in the fetish shrines and must be stopped. On the other hand, the priests were of the conviction that the practice was an integral part of the tradition and heritage of the Tongu people and could not be abolished.

INITIAL INTERVENTION STRATEGY– VOCATIONAL TRAINING PROGRAM

With the launch of the debate on the Trokosi issue in 1990, ING wrote a three-year proposal on the Trokosi Modernization Project through International Needs New Zealand, for funding by the New Zealand government. This project focused more on the vocational skills training aspect of the problem. The rationale for deciding to start the program with vocational skills training was twofold.

The first was to pull the Trokosi girls out of the shrines and to use the opportunity to offer psychological counseling and help them overcome the fear of death inculcated in them and which served as the major source of their bondage. Unlike traditional prisons with secure walls, fetish shrines do not have walls around them to prevent Trokosi slaves from running away. The Trokosi girls do not leave the shrines because they have been indoctrinated with the idea that if they leave the confines of the shrines, the wrath of the fetish will strike them dead.

The second reason for introducing vocational skills training was to provide the girls with employable skills which would enable them take care of themselves and their children. In November of 1991, the vocational training center was officially opened with 51 Trokosi girls from the North Tongu District. This first batch of Trokosi trainees were recruited by District Chief Executive, Clarke himself with the assistance of a quasi-political organization known as the cadres of the 31st December Revolution.

Prior to the establishment of the vocational training center, series of meetings were held with traditional rulers, quasi-political organizations and Trokosi practitioners in Tongu. In August 1991, a committee of chiefs and fetish priests submitted a landmark memorandum to the North Tongu District Assembly. The report read in part:

+ That the use of human beings [females] for pacifying the gods of the land [Tongu] for any form of offences committed is banned throughout the sub-region. And where a fetish should demand a human being for a sacrifice or as a pacifying agent, one fully developed and acceptable heifer and one ram should be accepted instead of the human being.

+ Those shrine inmates who have served their normal tenure of three years service in the shrines should unconditionally be released after the normal rites are performed in the shrines.

+ Those whose services are yet to come to an end could equally benefit from the new deal by giving out one heifer and one ram towards their release.

+ That the old practice whereby another young virgin girl termed 'akpexoxo-nuvuvu' replaces a deceased inmate should cease henceforth and in place one ram should be offered to the fetish priest and his elders.

+ That no secret rites should be performed in the shrines that would result in the taking on of human beings as Trokosis. And that all fetish priests and elders should ensure the fullest and strictest compliance of the above directives.

+ That any fetish priest who violates any of the directives should be prosecuted and fined in the sum of five hundred thousand cedis ($50) or in default to five year's imprisonment or both.

* With immediate effect, all customary rites/performances pertaining to the use of human beings [Trokosi] for pacifying the gods for crimes committed by relatives is totally prohibited throughout the district. (Memorandum from Chiefs, 1991, p. 2)

The biggest setback for this monumental step was that the fetish priests who were part of the committee refused to endorse the resolution and the report. Even though the compensation package appeared to be expensive ING was bearing the cost on behalf of the victims and families.

From 1992 to 1994, most of the activities of the Trokosi Modernization Project were concentrated around the vocational training center established at Adidome by ING. Taking some of the Trokosi girls out of the shrines and housing them at vocational training centers proved a worthy strategy indeed. Gradually, the Trokosi girls started opening up and telling of their horrifying experiences in the shrines. ING took the opportunity to invite both local and international media to publish the plight of the Trokosi girls. The publications resulted in an outcry from the general public demanding the abolition of the Trokosi system. The regularity, consistency and passion of the discourse, both in the print and electronic media resulted in organizations, such as the Federation of Women Lawyers, the National Commission on Women and Development (NCWD), and the Ghana National Commission on Children (GNCC), to send investigators to the field for verification. The Parliament of Ghana and the Commission on Human Rights and Administrative Justice also conducted independent investigations into the Trokosi system and came to the conclusion that the Trokosi system flagrantly violates various articles of the Constitution of Ghana and international human rights conventions that Ghana has ratified. Armed with reports of their various independent investigations, the above institutions joined ING in condemning the Trokosi practice and calling on the government to pass a specific law criminalizing the practice.

LAUNCH OF THE TROKOSI MODERNIZATION PROGRAM

In March of 1994, the Royal Danish Embassy funded the Trokosi Modernization Project with all the initial components. This timely support enabled ING to expand its work to fully cover human rights education and direct negotiation with the priests and shrine elders. In the same year, ING entered into a strategic working relationship with the Commission on Human Rights and Commission on Civic Education. The objective of the alliance was to ensure that all Trokosi-practicing communities were provided with human rights education to enable them to voluntarily put an end to the Trokosi system and other dehumanizing cultural practices. Four key individuals contributed immensely in pushing the Trokosi human rights education program forward: Emile Francis Short, the Commissioner of Human Rights and Administrative Justice; Mama Adokua Asigble IV, Queen mother of the Tefle Traditional area, and Member of the Commission on Civic Education; Rev. Walter Pimpong, the executive director of ING; and Wisdom Mensah the Projects Coordinator of ING (also the co-author of this book). While Commissioner Short and Mama Adokua Asigble IV distinguished themselves as chief educators, Mensah, provided advocacy and negotiation strategies and Rev. Pimpong had general oversight of the program.

HUMAN RIGHTS EDUCATION AND
FIRST NATIONAL WORKSHOP ON TROKOSI SYSTEM IN GHANA

The human rights education program took the participants to all six traditional areas of the North Tongu District. The program was in the form of seminars and durbars. While the seminars were held for targeted audiences (such as assembly members, village elders, queen mothers, fetish priests, and shrine elders), the durbars were generally held for community members. The seminars culminated in the organization of the first national workshop on the Trokosi system in Ghana in July 1995. The national workshop drew participants from the NGO sector, civil service, United Nations institutions, universities, Parliament, district assemblies, women's organizations, media, traditional rulers, and Trokosi practitioners. The recommendations of the workshop were as follows:

+ That the Trokosi practice emanated from the belief and religion of the people and the solution could best be found in education rather than legislation. It was recommended that vigorous education be pursued to bring about change. Literacy, both formal and informal, should also be pursued in Trokosi-practicing communities to bring enlightenment to the population.

+ That there were no accurate statistics on the fetish slaves and their dependents. Figures at best were estimates. The degree of harm inflicted on the girls (economically, socially and health wise) should be properly assessed and documented. A multidisciplinary approach should be adopted in the research.

+ Poverty, malnutrition and illiteracy, which are directly linked to Trokosi in the practicing communities, should be vigorously tackled. The fetish slave girls should be counseled, trained in vocational skills, and rehabilitated.

+ The fetish priests should be rehabilitated. A program should be created to make them productive citizens in their communities.

+ All stakeholders should cooperate in finding a lasting solution to the problem. (ING, 2001, p. 41)

Armed with the above recommendations, ING commissioned Professor Elom Dovlo of the Department for the Study of Religions at the University of Ghana, Legon, to conduct a study into the Trokosi institution. This study, the first of its kind, was completed in October of 1995. The report of the study was widely circulated and used as a tool for advocacy on the Trokosi issue. The study found the Trokosi institution to constitute gender discrimination, physical abuse, sexual abuse, child abuse, legal abuse, and spiritual bondage.

SEMINARS AND COMMUNITY DURBARS

After the first national workshop on the Trokosi system, human rights education on the Trokosi system was expanded beyond the North Tongu District to cover the remaining six Trokosi-practicing districts of South Tongu, Dangme East, Dangme West, Akatsi, Ketu, and Keta Districts. Series of seminars were organized at the various district capitals first for district assembly members, followed by seminars for traditional rulers and for fetish priests and their shrine elders. Some notable chiefs were recruited as facilitators of the seminars for the fetish priests and shrine elders. The next levels of educational programs were organized in the communities in the form of durbars. The district offices of the National Commission on Civic Education and Center for National Culture were used to reach community members at the grassroots level.

THE USE OF FM RADIO STATIONS IN HUMAN RIGHTS EDUCATION

In early 1996, ING extended its human rights advocacy program to cover the use of FM radio stations in the Volta Region. Once a week and for a period of one year, the ING Projects Coordinator and Advocacy officer addressed an aspect of the Trokosi issue on Volta FM Radio in the local dialect. The radio program, coupled with the community durbars, created a high level of awareness on the dehumanizing aspects of the Trokosi system. The radio programs also generated a lot of debate among community members, resulting in some Trokosi girls demanding their freedom and defying the orders of their shrine priests.

DIRECT TALKS AND NEGOTIATIONS WITH TROKOSI PRACTITIONERS

Within the same period, Wisdom Mensah, the ING Projects Coordinator, and Professor Elom Dovlo of the University of Ghana, formed a committee to engage in direct talks with fetish priests and shrine elders to negotiate the emancipation of the Trokosi women. The success of the talks depended on many factors, including knowledge of the background of the priest and his elders, and the ability to identify and lobby those who held real power in the shrine, chiefs and opinion leaders respected by priests and elders. After several efforts of negotiating the emancipation of the Trokosi women at various shrines, the Dada Piem shrine of Big Ada agreed to set their women free in July of 1996. The first shrine to take such a historical step was provided with a handsome rehabilitation package of 10 heifers and one bull given to the shrine priest and elders. ING made sure that both print and electronic media covered the emancipation ceremony. As expected, the rehabilitation package motivated other shrine practitioners to resolve to set their Trokosi women free.

LIBERATION CEREMONIES

During the first successful direct talks and negotiation meetings with the priests and shrine elders of the Dada Piem of Big Ada, a pattern was established. The first step was for the shrine priest and elders to put into writing a resolution denouncing the practice of Trokosi. The resolution contained the following:

+ A pledge to liberate the Trokosi women spiritually, psychologically, economically and physically, as well as their families and descendants for all time.
+ A vow to no longer accept human beings as objects of reparation.
+ A request for financial assistance to liberate the Trokosi girls held as servants in their shrines and a request for shrine rehabilitation in the form of an economic activity.

The second step was to provide the shrine with financial assistance by which time a list of Trokosi girls in servitude would be released to ING for verification and psychosocial, emotional and vocational assessment. The third step was to agree on a date to conduct pre-liberation counseling for the Trokosi women and to agree on a date for the public liberation ceremony. The program for the occasion was drawn up and invitations sent out. On the day of liberation, invited dignitaries and sponsors gave speeches, followed by the signing of legal documents by fetish priest, shrine elders, International Needs Ghana executives and the Commissioner for Human Rights and Administrative Justice. The fetish priests said traditional prayers, and emancipation rites were performed to publicly free the Trokosi women.

The importance of the public emancipation rituals cannot be overemphasized. The public pronouncements vows, prayers, and pledges of the fetish priests to set the Trokosi women free forever provided assurance to both families and Trokosi victims. It also gave the general public the opportunity to identify the shrine priests and monitor their future activities. The public pronouncements and prayers of the priests were enough commitment and spiritual sanction to ensure that the priests would not return to the Trokosi practice.

International Advocacy

While efforts were going on within Ghana to emancipate the Trokosi girls and outlaw the practice, ING also kick-started an international advocacy program to assist in the liberation of the Trokosi women. Part of the strategy was to invite all the world's major television stations to highlight the plight of the Trokosi girls. Notable among the international television stations that aired the Trokosi story across the globe were CBS, BBC, CNN, and MNET. In addition, ING sponsored a number of Trokosi women to travel abroad to international conferences to tell their own stories. Pressure was also brought to bear on the government of Ghana to promulgate a law criminalizing the Trokosi practice. This pressure came from international human rights organizations which at various times, sent petitions and action letters to the President and Parliament of Ghana to enforce international human rights instruments that Ghana has ratified.

Conclusion

Outreach using opinion leaders, chiefs, priests and the general public garnered the needed awareness to turn public opinion against the practice. The use of the local institutions and existing channels of communication enhanced the education drive and ensured that the message reached a large spectrum of people. The use of radio also provided a platform for dialogue and challenge of the status quo. The incentive package designed for the priests and shrine elders in a sense compensated them for the loss of income and the labor as a consequence of freeing the Trokosis. The liberation ceremonies were broadcast on radio and television thus putting pressure on the priests and shrine elders not to go back and practice in secret. In addition, they gave their word in public and undertook to sign a document of release. The involvement of the priests and shrine elders in the emancipation process—from verification of number of Trokosis, through pre-liberation counseling to the setting of dates for public emancipation ensured that all parties were on board. The performance of the public emancipation rites was a huge psycho-religious move. In the sense that the Trokosis, their families and the general public had great fear in the ability of the priests to cause harm to them, therefore witnessing them publicly renounce their hold on the Trokosis boosted confidence in the whole emancipation process. Thus, through a combination of direct talks, negotiations, rehabilitations, sustained interest, determination, education, psycho-spiritual approaches; local and international advocacy, and mounting political pressure, major steps were taken towards dismantling the Trokosi system.

CHAPTER 5

REHABILITATION OF

EMANCIPATED TROKOSI

INTRODUCTION

ALTHOUGH THE TROKOSI REHABILITATION EFFORTS by individuals and various institutions are commendable, the emancipation process requires critical examination in view of the problems some liberated Trokosi are facing. The process of liberating the women and children in bondage is a lengthy one. Advocacy and awareness measures require that all stakeholders in the system be appropriately consulted, sensitized, and addressed psycho-spiritually.

COUNSELING AND OUTREACH

With the emancipation of the first batch of Trokosi women in July 1996 came the second phase of ING's Trokosi Modernization Program. This second phase involved dealing with the psychosocial, emotional, and vocational needs and traumatic past of the emancipated Trokosi women. Dr. Bill Pupulampu, a consulting psychologist, was contracted to provide leadership in this aspect of the work. His task was to provide preliberation and postliberation counseling and follow-up services lasting for two years to the emancipated Trokosi women and their children, to assess their emotional and physical needs, and help resettle the women and their children.

As part of the rehabilitation program, facilities at the ING vocational training center were expanded to include a refuge center where those liberated Trokosi women who for one reason or the other could not rejoin their families could be housed and taken care of. Although families accepted the majority of the emancipated Trokosi women and their children back home, most of them lacked the basic necessities of life, including clothing, food, and shelter. Therefore ING provided for those needs. In addition to meeting the basic needs of the women and their children, ING gave each emancipated Trokosi woman seed capital with which to start life as a free independent person. ING also facilitated the mainstreaming of Trokosi children into basic schools. These children continue to enjoy educational sponsorship from International Needs Ghana.

Although the sustained advocacy program resulted in the emancipation of thousands of women and children from servitude, there was a dire need to provide sustainable training packages for the women. The three-year vocational skills training program in dressmaking, kente weaving, and hairdressing were shortened to a three-month modular skills training program with emphasis on high-income-generating skills such as batik, tie and dye making, mat weaving as well as bread and confectionaries making, pomade, soap and powder making. With the modular vocational training program in place, ING was able to train a maximum of 300 women in a year.

Upon the completion of the skills training program, each graduate was equipped with a set of working tools that guaranteed the smooth commencement of an income-generating activity in a chosen vocation. For instance, a graduate in bread baking is given two bags of flour, a bag of sugar, a bucket of margarine, and spices. In addition, she is provided with an amount of money as seed capital, and an earthen oven, which is constructed in her community. Care is taken to ensure that the tools used could be supported by the local industry so that maintenance would not be a problem.

To ensure sustainability of the income-generating activities of the emancipated Trokosi women and to guarantee their access to credit, a microcredit program was established by ING in 1998 with funding from the Australian government through International Needs Australia. Since the establishment of the program, hundreds of ex-Trokosi women have benefited from it.

SEXUAL AND REPRODUCTIVE HEALTH EDUCATION

It is an open secret that one of the tenets of Trokosi is sexual promiscuity and sexual abuse of women in servitude. For instance, in Afife where there are 5 Fiashidi shrines, there is a festival each year during which all Trokosi women are encouraged to engage in sexual intercourse with other men. This practice is called "dodese" literally translated as: taboo on the vagina is lifted. This means that during the festival any man could have sex with a Trokosi without incurring the wrath of the gods. The majority of the Trokosi women, therefore, have sexual attitudes that need to be evaluated after their emancipation to enable them to live normal lives. In view of these issues and HIV/AIDS pandemic in Ghana, ING invited the Planned Parenthood Association of Ghana (PPAG) to assist in organizing sexual and reproductive health education including information on HIV/AIDS and sexually transmitted diseases, in Trokosi-practicing communities and the vocational training center, as part of the counseling and rehabilitation program. In addition to the educational programs, PPAG offered services, such as clinics and the sale of condoms, to the ex-Trokosi women and community members.

SECOND NATIONAL WORKSHOP

By 1998, over 1,000 Trokosi women had been liberated and the cumulative experience gained working with the emancipated women generated the need for sharing knowledge, information, and best practices with a wider community through a national workshop. So the Second National workshop on the Trokosi system in Ghana was organized under the auspices of ING. The workshop sought, among other goals, to do the following:

+ To create a forum to report back to stakeholders and partners on progress made so far in dismantling the Trokosi system.
+ To afford the public the opportunity to know more about specific strategies adopted to emancipate and rehabilitate liberated Trokosi victims.
+ To create the forum for stakeholders to share ideas on best practices with ING on how to achieve more success in the Trokosi Modernization Project.

The major recommendations of the workshop were as follows:

+ The Trokosi practice constituted a gross violation of human rights and freedoms of the victims, and the practice should be abolished.
+ Parliament was urged to expedite action on the bill that would criminalize the Trokosi system.

+ Dialogue should continue to be used as an effective means of communication to bring change.

+ Continued human rights education and negotiations were critical to ensuring that the practice does not go underground.

+ Shrine owners and priests, including opinion leaders in affected communities, should be primary targets for education.

+ Opinion leaders in affected communities who were sympathetic to change should be used to reach their communities for change.

+ Awareness should be disseminated broadly beyond the boarders of Ghana to countries with similar practices and challenges.

+ The government needs to make enforceable laws, coupled with efficient law enforcement.

+ NGOs, women's groups, churches, government, interested groups and individuals should contribute to a fund set up to deal with the Trokosi issue.

+ ING should continue to play a coordinating role of all actors in the Trokosi project in order to prevent duplication of efforts. (British Council, 1998)

For all intents and purposes, the workshop was a success, in that it broadened the conversation, helped to focus attention on the critical areas, created greater awareness of the plight of the Trokosis and popularized the rehabilitation program.

Coupled with the lobby and pressure of civil society organizations, the media and international human rights organizations, was the role played by individual ex-Trokosi girls. Juliana Dorgbadzi and Mercy Senahe are two worthy of mention. It is on record that Juliana Dorgbadzi presented a strong case in Parliament and other local and international fora and also wrote a letter to then President of the Republic of Ghana, Jerry Rawlings, appealing to him to pass a legislation criminalizing the

Trokosi system. Mercy Senahe, traveled to the United Kingdom to speak to the British Parliament, to The Hague (World Court of Justice), and to South Africa to speak on the Trokosi issue. All these efforts in no small way resulted in the decision of Ghana's Executive and Legislator to pass the law, prohibiting the practice.

CUSTOMARY SERVITUDE PROHIBITION LAW

One of the beauties of collaborating with several civil society organizations in advocating for the modernization of the Trokosi system is the multiplier effect their combined pressure had on the government. The pressure and the lobby of government functionaries resulted in the promulgation of the Criminal Code (Amendment) Act, 1998. The Act amended the Criminal Code Act 29 by the insertion of section 314A entitled 'Prohibition of Customary Servitude.' The new section states:

1. Whoever -
   a) sends to or receives at any place any person; or
   b) participates in or is concerned in any ritual or customary activity in respect of any person with the purpose of subjecting that person to any form of ritual or customary servitude or any form of forced labor related to a customary ritual commits an offence and shall be liable on conviction to imprisonment for a term not less than three years.
2. In this section "to be concerned in" means -
   a) to send to, take to, consent to the taking to or receive at any place any person for the performance of the customary ritual; or
   b) to enter into any agreement whether written or oral to subject any of the parties to the agreement or any other person to the performance of the customary ritual; or

c) to be present at any activity connected with or related to the performance of the customary ritual.

However, it is sad to note that despite the passage of the law, the enforcement agencies have not been able to muster the will to ensure compliance. The law therefore remains a piece of decoration on Ghana's statute books.

LEGAL EDUCATION

On the other hand the passage of the "Prohibition of Customary Servitude" law has been of tremendous help to the educational campaign of ING. In addition to the International Human Rights Instruments and the Constitution of Ghana, which were used as the basis for community education on the evils of the Trokosi system, the law criminalizing Trokosi became another persuasive legal means to change the attitudes and perceptions of practitioners and community members.

Workshops and seminars were organized to educate the public, especially members of the Trokosi-practicing communities. Every Trokosi community was reached with education on the law. Assembly members in Ketu, Akatsi, North Tongu, South Tongu, and Dangme East District (critical areas with a high concentration of Trokosi shrines) were all educated. The police and heads of all government organizations in the aforementioned districts where Trokosi is practiced were also targeted with legal education. Commissioner Emile Short and the Volta Regional police commander were among resource persons at the seminars and workshops.

Most of the Trokosi shrines in the Akatsi District resolved to end the practice of Trokosi as a result of the legal advocacy conducted after the law was passed. Out of the 3,000 Trokosi women emancipated by 2002, about 1,500 were liberated after the passage of the law, an indication that the law has a useful purpose to serve, after all. The passage of the law also heightened sharply the opposition to the Trokosi modernization campaign by a section of Ewe communities who call themselves traditionalists.

First West African Workshop
on Female Ritual Servitude

After the passage of the law criminalizing Trokosi and other customary servitude practices in Ghana, reports from the field indicated that some of the Trokosi priests close to the Togo border were contemplating moving their shrines into Togo. Those who had already emancipated their Trokosi women were also showing signs of opening fresh shrines in neighboring countries if the legal environment in those countries was favorable. There was, therefore, a new danger of the Trokosi practitioners going underground and resurfacing in neighboring countries. This workshop was clearly a follow-up to one of the recommendations of the second national workshop on the Trokosi system in Ghana, where participants recommended that civil society and human rights organizations, including the relevant government agencies of Togo and Benin, be brought together to deal with the issue. The field reports, coupled with some of the recommendations of the Second National Workshop on the Trokosi System in Ghana, became the bases for organizing a sub-regional conference on the issue of female ritual servitude, still under the auspices of ING.

In February of 2001, the first-ever West African sub-regional workshop on female ritual servitude was organized in Accra with sponsorship from Global Ministries of United States of America and Anti-Slavery International of the United Kingdom.

The purpose of the workshop was threefold:

+ To create a forum for interaction and sharing of information and experience for civil society and human rights organizations fighting against female ritual servitude.

+ To initiate strategic alliances and partnerships between various government institutions and civil society organizations with the aim of fostering future cooperation in the eradication of female ritual servitude.

+ To create strategies and follow-up programs towards the transformation of Fiashidi/Trokosi and other forms of ritual servitude of women in the West African sub region. (ING, 2001)

There were 70 participants representing government agencies, parliamentarians, civil society organizations, human rights groups, and Trokosi shrine priests from Benin, Togo, and Ghana. At the end of the workshop, participants made the following resolutions:

+ That participants from Benin, Togo, and Ghana embark on intensive sensitization campaigns on the practice of female ritual servitude at the community, national, and sub-regional levels.

+ That participants form the nucleus of alliances to advocate the passing and implementation of legislations against practices of female ritual servitude.

+ That each country in the sub-region generates an action plan to combat practices of female ritual servitude in their various countries.

+ That participants continue to network to meet the common objective of transforming and eradicating practices of female ritual servitude in the sub regions.

+ That participants share information on the transformation and eradication of female ritual servitude through print and electronic media to the mutual benefit of Anglophone and Francophone countries in the sub region. (ING, 2001)

These conclusions were certainly historical and, to a large extent, created the right atmosphere for networking and cooperation.

OPPOSITION FROM AFRIKANIA MISSION

Despite all the good work going on and the outcry against the inhumanity of the practice of Trokosi, there were some voices of opposition maintaining that the practice was cultural and should not be interfered with. Mention has already been made of some opposition from priests and traditionalists, but chief among the opponents of the Trokosi modernization campaign has been traditional believers who belong to a group called Afrikania mission led by Kofi Ameve (now deceased). They assert that Trokosi is an integral part of the way of life of traditional Ewe communities and a major pillar of the Ewe culture. Their mode of operation has been to counter every publication on the Trokosi issue, be it through the newspapers, radio, or television. By countering the efforts of pro-emancipation activists, Afrikania Mission was able to convince some of the shrine priests to continue the Trokosi practice. These shrines have formed an umbrella group called the Council of Troxovi Shrines. They are headquartered in Klikor in the Volta Region. Klikor is a village that has 3 major shrines with several hundreds of Fiashidi women.

CONTROVERSY OVER THE NUMBER OF VICTIMS

According to a baseline study conducted in 1997 by Elom Dovlo and Sosthenes Kufogbe of the University of Ghana, there were about 2,000 more women in Trokosi servitude. However, another survey by Nukunya (1997a &1997b), an anthropologist and one time pro-vice

Chancellor (Provost) of the University of Ghana, indicated that the number of incarcerated Trokosi women was still over 8,000. On the other hand, the 2002 Democracy and Human Rights Report of the U.S. Department of State indicated that the number of women in Trokosi servitude in Ghana was fewer than 100.

Since there was no authoritative source of data on the exact number of Trokosi victims in Ghana, International Needs Ghana, with funding from the Canadian International Development Agency (CIDA) in 1997, commissioned a Baseline Survey on the Geographic Spread and Count of Victims of the Trokosi practice in Ghana (Dovlo & Kufogbe, 1997). Other organizations that undertook studies on Trokosi include FESLIM and SENTINEL. Other sources of data are unpublished essays and theses, newspaper publications, unpublished reports, and the archives of International Needs (Ghana). The CIDA report is therefore the only authoritative source of data on the estimate of Trokosi in the country.

Apart from the CIDA project, there is no elaborate methodology for assessing the number of Trokosi victims. The methodology adopted for the CIDA project survey involved both primary and secondary sources of data. The primary data sources involved the shrines, their localities, officiating priests/priestesses, and victims of the practice. These were identified either directly through personal contact or indirectly through informants, notably heads of families, traditional rulers (chiefs and queenmothers), government officials, and opinion leaders. This method was adopted because of the secrecy in which the phenomenon is shrouded, and fear which people, especially natives and devotees, attach to the power of the gods to punish and even kill traitors who divulge secrets of the practice to "outsiders."

Other methodologies adopted to study the Trokosi practice by other authors include participant observation, as adopted by Romanoff (1999), who studied the Trokosi system at Klikor, a community famous for the practice. She concentrated solely on Klikor without studying other practices elsewhere. She also did not attempt a count of the victims.

The 2002 International Religious Freedom Report released by the U.S. Bureau of Democracy, Human Rights, and Labor also attempted to show the number of victims under Trokosi. However, this report did not elaborate on the methodology used to arrive at the number of Trokosi victims. The Department of State report only noted that:

> In September 2001, Embassy officers conducted a survey of Trokosi shrines, which included four separate trips to the Volta Region and nearly 2 weeks in the field, along with extensive interviews of government officials, foreign Embassy officers, religious leaders, shrine priests, NGO representatives, members of civil society, and Trokosis themselves. Embassy officials identified no more than 2 dozen active Trokosi shrines in the Volta Region, with a total of fewer than 100 girls serving their atonement periods. (U.S. Department of State, 2009)

A major shortcoming of the United States Embassy report is the inability to count those who have completed their atonement period and are no longer at the shrines but periodically give allegiance to the shrine and the deities.

However available studies indicate that the catchment area of the practice extends beyond the borders of Ghana into Togo and Benin (Dovlo & Kufogbe, 1997; Nukunya & Kwafo, 1999b). Data provided by this study reveal that there are over 51 shrines scattered in over 30 different communities across seven districts in southeastern Ghana. The research estimated that there are more than 4,714 women in bondage. The Volta, Greater Accra, and Eastern regions constitute the catchment regions in Ghana, with the Volta Region having the highest concentration of the practice. There are no clearly defined Trokosi institutions in the other regions of the country.

In addition to the estimates above, another point that makes the conclusion of the United States Department of State report unfortunate is that an organization called Every Child Ministries (ECM) reported on their web site that as of December 2006, they had been instrumental in organizing three liberations which ended the practice of slavery in five shrines and freed 1,000 slaves and 4,000 of their children. The modus operandi of ECM is very similar to that of ING. For example they help liberated Trokosis to rebuild their broken lives by assisting them to obtain vocational training and start small businesses. They also have compensation packages for the priests and public liberation ceremonies. They estimate that it amounted to $200 to actually free an average of five people (Every Child Ministries, n.d.).

This palpable disparity in the population of women in servitude has not only contributed to fueling attacks on the work of ING and partners, but it has also become a major source of confusion and greatly damaged the credibility of ING's work. For instance, in the year 2000, as a result of the less than 100 figure declared by the United States Department of State report, the African Development Foundation had to cancel a $500,000 grant to expand microfinance facilities to the Trokosi women and practicing communities in the Volta Region.

CONCLUSION

Despite the setbacks recounted above, it is the strong conviction of the authors that change, which is an inevitable phenomenon, will slowly but surely happen within the Trokosi system. Too many good things have already happened to prevent the wheels of change from grinding to a halt.

CHAPTER 6

THE ROLE OF CIVIL SOCIETY IN CONFRONTING TROKOSI

INTRODUCTION

IT HAS BECOME EVIDENT THAT the government of Ghana, NGOs, and civil society at large has roles to play in advocating the emancipation of Trokosi girls. Members of civil society should be encouraged and supported to do the things that they have comparative leverage to do to help in the liberation of Trokosis.

DEFINING CIVIL SOCIETY

Civil society can generally be described as any association outside the state apparatus. Cohen and Arator (1992) see civil society as all organizations outside the state and family formed by citizens where people associate across ties of kinship, aside from the market. These associations generally remain independent of the state in order to play the role of watchdogs effectively. Naidoo and Tandon (1999) on the

71

other hand view civil society as the "network of autonomous associations rights-bearing and responsibility-laden citizens voluntarily created to address common problems, advance shared interests, and promote collective aspirations" (p. 7). Thus civil society is characterized by independence from government, driven by specific aims for the collective good. Another definition rendered by Rojas (1999) drives home the view point of autonomy from the state; it states that civil society is "organized voluntarily as opposed to being organized through the coercive apparatus of the state" (p. 88). Civil society therefore becomes the platform to register concerns about state/local policies that affect the common good of society and the pivot around which society and community groups mobilize themselves. Thus in confronting the entrenched Trokosi system, civil society organizations rose to the challenge.

ROLE OF CHIEFTAINCY INSTITUTION

Since the Trokosi issue came to the public's attention two decades ago, civil society has played a vanguard role in providing solutions. The activists include the Association of Queenmothers, Council of Chiefs, and NGOs. For instance the Tongu Association of Queenmothers, a recognized traditional authority in the Tongu area, campaigned strongly against the Trokosi system. They were one of the first groups within civil society to organize face-to-face meetings with Tongu Trokosi practitioners. They were also articulate in highlighting the gender inequalities inherent in the Trokosi system. As part of their advocacy efforts, the Association sent a number of petitions to the government calling on it to enact appropriate legislation to modify the Trokosi system. Worthy of mention is the dynamic role of Nana Adokuwa Asigble IV, the queenmother of Tefle traditional area in the Volta region and president of the Tongu Association of Queenmothers. As a member of the National Commission on Civic Education, she left no stone unturned in advocating the modification of the Trokosi system.

The council of paramount chiefs of the various Trokosi-practicing districts also played significant roles in the quest for a solution to the Trokosi issue. As custodians of culture, most of the traditional rulers were involved in advocacy and community sensitization programs to educate Trokosi practitioners and community members to stop the Trokosi system. The Tongu paramount chiefs were the first to propose a solution to the Trokosi issue. Although this resolution was not implemented due to the resistance of the Trokosi priests and their elders, the resolution pointed to the fact that there was, indeed, a possible solution. It is also important to note that future intervention strategies drew a lot of inspiration from this first resolution.

The landmark resolution dated August 2, 1991 stated among other things:

- That the paramount chiefs, the sub-chiefs, their elders and entire people of Tongu should set aside a day on which elaborate customary rites would be performed to transform practices connected with fetish shrines in the sub-region (Tongu), i.e., pour libation to the gods that day making changes in the cultural practices connected with the fetish shrines.
- That the North Tongu District Administration, for that matter, the District Assembly, in collaboration with affiliated Non-Governmental Organizations which shared similar sentiments as the committee on this sort of dehumanizing cultural practices, should provide items/money for the rites to be performed at Adidome on Saturday November 23, 1991.
- That with the performance of these customary rites backed by the enactment of a by-law by the District Assembly on the use of human

beings (females) for pacifying the gods of the land (Tongu) for any form of offences committed is banned throughout the Tongu sub-region. Where a fetish should demand a human being as a pacifying agent, one fully developed and acceptable heifer and one ram should be accepted instead of a human being.

+ That 'inmates' of the shrines who have served their normal tenure of three years service in the shrines should unconditionally be released after the normal rites were performed in the shrine.

+ That those whose services are yet to come to an end could equally benefit from the new deal by giving out one heifer and one ram towards their release.

+ That the old practice, whereby, a deceased 'inmate' is replaced by another young lady should cease henceforth and in her place one ram should be offered to the fetish priest and his elders.

+ That no secret rites should be performed in the shrines that would result in the taking on of human beings as Trokosi. And that all fetish priests and their elders should ensure the fullest and strictest compliance of the above directives. That any fetish priest who violates any of these directives should be prosecuted and fined in the sum of ¢ 0.5millon (equivalent to $50) or in default to five years imprisonment or to both.

+ With immediate effect, all customary rites/performances pertaining to the use of human beings for pacifying the gods for crimes committed by a family member is totally prohibited throughout the district. (Resolution of Tongu Paramount Chiefs and Queenmothers, 1991, p. 2)

Role of NGO's and International Organizations

NGOs that blew the whistle against the Trokosi system included both local and international NGOs. Among the local NGOs that campaigned vigorously against the Trokosi practice were International Needs Ghana

(ING), Missions International, and Fetish Slaves Liberation Movement (FESLIM). While Missions International and FESLIM were outspoken in the early stages of the campaign (between 1990 and 1996), it was ING that launched an all-out assault on the system, resulting in the emancipation and rehabilitation of over 3,000 Trokosi slaves and their children. On the international scene, NGOs such as Equality Now, Anti-Slavery International, and international media houses, such as CNN, BBC, and CBS, were very instrumental in disseminating information about the Trokosi issue. Their efforts drew the world's attention to the issue and resulted in the international community putting pressure on the government of Ghana.

ING's efforts were more of a holistic approach to the issue and included an aggressive advocacy and community sensitization program on the Trokosi, as well as sustained domestic and international media coverage to keep the Trokosi issue in the public eye and on the human rights agenda. ING was also involved in direct negotiations with Trokosi practitioners resulting in the liberation of the Trokosi women and the rehabilitation of both the Trokosi priests and emancipated women. Their rehabilitation programs included provision of psychosocial, emotional, and vocational counseling of the women; vocational skills training and provision of tools; microcredit programs; and the provision of resettlement items, including clothing and sometimes housing.

The financial and moral support of international development and bilateral institutions, such as the Danish International Development Agency, New Zealand Government Development Fund, United States Human Rights Fund, Australian Government Development Aid, United Nations Development Program, United Nations Fund for Population Activities, United Nations Children and Emergency Fund, United Nations Development Fund for Women, and International Needs in Europe and America, greatly helped in mounting a sustained advocacy and educational program on the Trokosi issue and rehabilitating liberated Trokosi women and their children. The Danish International Development Agency was the first to provide assistance to emancipate, rehabilitate, and fully integrate back into society the first one thousand Trokosi women and their children.

CONCLUSION

The efforts of the government of Ghana in dealing with the Trokosi issue have been very marginal. The major achievement has been the passage of legislation in 1998 criminalizing customary servitude which includes the Trokosi issue. For full text of the law, see chapter 5, Customary Servitude Prohibition Law. However, beyond the passage of the law, little or no effort has been made to enforce the law by bringing culprits to justice, securing the freedom or rehabilitating of the Trokosi victims. Part of the inability of government functionaries, especially the police, to enforce the law is attributed to their belief in the supernatural power of the Trokosi deities to kill anyone who attempts to dismantle the practice by bringing perpetrators to justice. The potency of the law has also been weakened by the utterances of highly respected politicians and academicians who condemn the law as an infringement on the cultural heritage of the people.

The efforts of two national independent bodies in Ghana are worthy of mention and commendation. These bodies include the Commission on Human Rights and Administrative Justice and the National Commission on Civic Education. These two commissions formed a strategic alliance with International Needs Ghana to conduct advocacy and community educational programs in Trokosi-practicing communities, ultimately resulted in the emancipation of over 3,000 of Trokosi women and their children. Their official public pronouncement and appeals to government to abolish the practice contributed immensely to exerting pressure on the government to enact legislation outlawing the Trokosi practice. The efforts of the local media; radio, newspapers and television contributed in no small measure to exposing, informing, and educating the general public on the Trokosi issue. The media greatly helped in dislodging the myth of fear and invincibility that surrounded the Trokosi issue.

CHAPTER 7

THE DISCOURSES

INTRODUCTION

THE TROKOSI SYSTEM IS A violation of various fundamental human rights that are enshrined not only in the 1992 Constitution of Ghana, but also in other regional and international human rights instruments, such as the United Nations Convention on the Rights of the Child. To many, the Trokosi system is a flagrant violation of human rights. To others Trokosi is a display of gender inequality with impunity—a practice which seeks to reduce the female gender to a state of perpetual servitude. The system of Trokosi can also be looked at from the perspective of patriarchy, a perpetuation of male chauvinism and a class society. The authors assert however, that Trokosi is an amalgamation of several or all of the above perspectives and wish to analyze some of the perspectives separately.

CULTURAL RELATIVISM OR UNIVERSALISM

Although there is disagreement regarding the categorization of Trokosi as a human rights issue, this chapter argues that the issue of

Trokosi is a human rights issue and violates international, sub regional and national human rights norms. Although one school of thought asserts that the system of Trokosi falls under the universal principles of human rights, there are traditionalists who adhere to the view that Trokosi is part of the cultural heritage of the practicing ethnic groups and therefore should not be subjected to human rights norms. This sentiment is captured by An-na'im and Deng (1990) as follows:

> Some governments and elites from developing countries maintain that the current international human rights standards are not binding on them not only because the standards were conceived and formulated largely by Westerners, but also because they reflect cultural values and mores that are foreign to non-Western traditions and therefore antithetic to third world priorities. (p. xi)

The theories of universalism and cultural relativism are important for the discussion at this stage. The Universalist theory holds that "human rights are universal, reflecting the autonomous, individual nature of the human being" (Symonides, 2002, p. 56). According to An-na'im and Deng (1990), "the idea if not the content of human rights—as claims to which every person is entitled by virtue of being human—is founded on fundamental values that are shared by all cultural traditions" (p. xii).

Human rights norms according to An-na'im and Deng (1990) are universal because they are standards set by the international community under the United Nations Charter for every nation and peoples to aspire to and promote. These universal standards reflect the collective conscience and political will of the international community; they represent a higher order of human aspirations, with a more effective mechanism for promotion and enforcement.

The basic argument of the cultural relativist school is that there are no absolute human rights, that the "principles which we may use for judging behavior are relative to the society in which we are raised, that there is infinite cultural variability, and that all cultures are morally equal or valid" (Symonides, 2002, p. 56). The traditionalists in Ghana who oppose treating the Trokosi issue as a human rights issue maintain that the system has been an acceptable cultural practice of the ethnic groups in question for several centuries without any complaints. Goldtzamann confirms this notion by stating:

> Proponents of Trokosi emboldened by their spirituality argue that, it is a custom that has endured hundred of years and has severe religious repercussions…it has no economic incentives, but it is a deeply rooted religious belief and community practice. It is not brutality but justice being carried out on the terms of the gods. The priests are simply following the rules of their religious convictions as other religions require of their followers. (1998, p. 60)

While it is a fact that the United Nations Bill of Rights was formulated when sub-Saharan African countries, including Ghana, were not members of the United Nations, it is a misconception to say that human right is an unknown concept among non-Western countries. According to An-na'im and Deng the idea that human rights is alien to some cultural traditions may arise because some cultures do not articulate the values underlying these rights and also do not apply them to all human beings on an equal basis. Some cultural traditions tend to accord certain persons, such as women, minors, and outsiders, a lower status, thereby denying them the full range of claims to which the more privileged members of the society are entitled (1990, p. xii).

Those who oppose handling the Trokosi issue in Ghana as a human rights issue do so not because the culture does not articulate human rights values but because they perceive the status of women to be as low as that of animals. The authors are reliably informed that in some communities Trokosi girls are called goats because they are literally sacrificial lambs.

Interestingly, these values enshrined in the Universal Declaration of Human Rights are not called "Western rights" but "human rights." This essentially means that these rights are inseparable from a person's humanity. Those who oppose these do not do so from any perceived or real contradictions with cultural norms but for self-serving interests usually favoring a ruling class, for hegemonic values or other such parochial interests.

The concept of fundamental human rights transcends all cultures. According to Fennis (1990):

> All human societies' show a concern for the value of human life... in none is the killing of other human beings permitted without some fairly definite justification. In all societies there is some prohibition of incest, some opposition to boundless promiscuity and to rape, some favor for stability and permanence in sexual relations. All societies display a concern for truth; ... all societies display a favor for the values of cooperation, of common over individual good. All display a concern for powers or principles which are to be respected as supra-human. (ch. IV)

TROKOSI AND HUMAN RIGHTS

Human rights activists argue that Trokosi is a modern form of slavery in which girls/women are forced to serve the shrine, often from a very young age; and there are well-documented cases of forced labor and sexual abuse, as has been discussed in previous chapters. Traditional religious groups, however, claim it is nothing but a benign custom. ECM reports of stories of Trokosi victims recounting being given a choice between a whip and broken glasses when they refuse anything demanded by the priest. For example, when they do not make their work quota, or when they displease him in any way. Ironically it is the only choice ever offered. They can be whipped long and hard while others hold them down, or they can kneel for hours on large shards of broken glasses, with no medical care afterwards (Every Child Ministries, n.d.). How else can one explain this situation other than to call it what it is—abuse? The situation where the only time Trokosis get to make a choice or their opinion sought on an issue is to select from two abysmal options is devastating, untenable and bizarre. However the Afrikania Mission, an organization that represents most of the fetish shrines in the Volta Region of Ghana where the practice is prominent, champions the cause of the traditionalists and prefers to call Trokosi a tradition. What a sell out!

The Trokosi system violates fundamental human rights and freedoms as enshrined in the International Bill of Human Rights and in the Constitution of the Republic of Ghana. Article 12 section (2) of the Fourth Republican Constitution of Ghana guarantees the fundamental human rights and freedoms of every person in Ghana but subject to the respect of the rights and freedoms of others and for the public interest. The Trokosi system violates Article 15 of the Constitution of Ghana which provides that:

1. The dignity of all persons shall be inviolable
2. No person shall whether or not he is arrested, restricted or detained be subject to -
   a) torture or other cruel, inhuman or degrading treatment or punishment,
   b) any other condition that detracts or is likely to detract from his dignity and self worth as a human being.

The above article is echoed by Article 4 of the African Charter on Human and People's Rights to which Ghana is a signatory. This article states: "Human beings are inviolable. Every human being shall be entitled to respect for his life and the integrity of his person." A similar provision is found in the Universal Declaration of Human Rights Article 4 and 5 respectively. The Trokosi system also violates Article 16(1) and (2) of the Constitution of Ghana which provides that:

a) No person shall be held in slavery or servitude.
b) No person shall be required to perform forced labor.

Justice Emile Short, commissioner of the Ghana Human Rights Commission, had this to say in reference to the slavery inherent in the Trokosi system:

> The Trokosi system insofar as it requires the girls to minister to the needs of the shrine and priest by going as far as to cut down trees, burn charcoal, sweep the shrine, etc, against their will amounts to subjecting the Trokosis to slavery, servitude and forced labor, all of which are prohibited by Article 16 (1) and (2). (Short, 2001, p. 2)

ECM reports on its web site that Ghanaian officials speaking at liberation ceremonies for the Trokosi slaves have remarked that the tradition of Trokosi is the very worst form of child labor. Children are torn from school and family and forced into long, strenuous labor with inadequate food, no health care, and no moral support. They are stripped of dignity, humanity, and hope, as they are forced to labor in the priest's fields from morning till night with no recompense, thanks, encouragement, or recognition. It is difficult to think of a more cruel form of child labor, of a more devastating form of child abuse. Trokosi is a heinous abuse of Africa's youth. If indeed Africa's children are her greatest natural resource, we must conclude that the practice of Trokosi slavery is the deliberate spoilage of her greatest resource (Every Child Ministries, n.d.).

TROKOSI AND GENDER DISCRIMINATION

In this context gender refers to the socio-cultural constructed components of responsibilities attached to each male and female. Gender inequality, therefore, refers to sociocultural definitions of, and reactions to, biological sex that produce and reinforce inequality between males and females (Chafetz, 1990, p. 28). The Trokosi system hardly uses male children as objects of reparation but instead uses virgin girls to atone for crimes purported to have been committed by family members. According to Gadzekpo (1993) "Trokosi is an archaic and harsh criminal justice system; a system where male criminals pay for their crimes by offering female family members to serve the gods" (p. 5). Under normal circumstances, only girls are made to serve the shrine or deity, in rare cases boys are also offered (Nukunya & Kwafo, 1999a).

The reason that only girls are forced into Trokosi servitude as objects of reparation lies in the sociocultural roles assigned to women in the Ewe culture. These roles include, doing house chores, serving the male partner, working on the farm and providing reproductive and childcare services. Dovlo and Adzoyi (1995) have thrown more light on this issue by stating the following:

> One particular role of the Trokosi that has brought the institution to public opprobrium is the domestic and other services the Trokosi women render personally to the Trokosi priest. Their

84

duties to the priest include the performance of domestic chores such as cooking, washing and taking care of visitors and seeing to their overnight accommodation etc. The society is an agrarian society and the girls are used extensively to farm for the priests. They at times work from dawn to dusk. However, they are not remunerated. Neither do they share or partake of the farm produce of their labor, not even for domestic consumption. (p. 15)

In addition, girls or women are more prone to fear, on which the Trokosi system is based, for that matter, the priest of these shrines are aware that culturally it is more difficult for females to rebel. The males, on other hand, are more likely to revolt against the system. Therefore, the priests of these shrines keep girls and women as weaker vessels (Boateng, 2001). Furthermore, these Trokosi inmates are sent to the shrines at very tender ages and grow to accept their fate as natural; hence, they become part and parcel of the institution. As young women living with elderly men in a patriarchal society most of them are unable to resist the authority of these priests. They eventually settle into a life of discrimination and harassment where they are seen as mere objects.

The strategic choice of enslaving females and not males has other implications. One such implication is the free sexual service derived by cohabiting with the Trokosis. During several of the human rights sensitization sessions, witnesses quoted some priests as retorting that "if human rights activists do not want us to have sex with the girls, do they want us to sleep with goats?"

In confirming this fact, Dovlo and Adzoyi (1995) note:

Bondage goes beyond manual labor for the Trokosi. They are also required to sleep with the Tronua [Priest] at his behest. It is claimed that after the third menstruation the priest is entitled to sexual intercourse with the girls. The maiden may therefore begin to bear children at a tender age. The resultant problems of teenage pregnancy are there for all to see. Trokosi can therefore be labeled as ritual slavery and sexual bondage. Trokosi girls are denied the right to education by their benefactors although basic education is free and compulsory in Ghana. While there is an existing disparity between boy and girl child education, this disparity is worsened in the case of Trokosi girls who by their status are not allowed to go to school at all. One consequence of restricting the girls to the shrine and in servitude to farm for the priests is that they are denied access to education and other secular forms of training that would equip them for the modern world. (p. 11)

From the foregoing, one can conclude that the practice of Trokosi violates the spirit and letter of the Convention on the Elimination of All Forms of Discrimination Against Women (CEDAW) adopted in 1979 by the United Nations General Assembly. Part (1) Article (1) of the Convention defines discrimination against women as:

... Any distinction, exclusion or restriction made on the basis of sex which has the effect or purpose of impairing or nullifying the recognition, enjoyment or exercise by women, irrespective of their marital status, on a basis of equality of men and women, of human rights and fundamental freedoms in the political, economic, social, cultural, civil or any other field.

This article therefore echoes that discrimination of any form against women, denial of certain rights or limitations placed on them that compromises their equality of rights with men, is fundamentally unjust and constitutes an offence against human dignity. Article 1 encapsulates the spirit and letter of CEDAW that Trokosi flagrantly violates.

TROKOSI AND CHILD RIGHTS

Girls sent into Trokosi slavery are mostly between the ages of 6 and 13 years. From a strict ritualistic perspective, the girls are not supposed to start their menstruation before committal. They are also expected to be virgins. Most often these children begin primary education before they are withdrawn from school and sent into the shrines. It is also not uncommon to find that children sent into Trokosi ritual slavery are traumatized because of the tender age at which they are uprooted from their parents, peers, and communities of origin. Sometimes they are carried across national boundaries and from one ethnic group to another. It is commonplace for instance, to find Trokosi girls in the three shrines in Klikor (Ghana) hailing from Togo and Benin (two neighboring countries).

In fact, one of the co-authors facilitated the freedom of a seven year old girl in one of the shrines in the Ketu District of the Volta Region who was brought all the way from the village of Hasome between the middle portion of the Togo and Benin borders. She was removed from her village, which was an Ajah ethnic community, and from her school, which used French as a lingua franca, and brought to live among Ewe-speaking peoples whose lingua franca was English. This child felt confused, lost and handicapped with limited linguistic abilities.

The foregoing facts are indicative of the violation of the Rights of the Child as provided for in various sections of the United Nations Convention on the Rights of the Child. It is ironic that while Ghana prides itself as the first country on earth to ratify the United Nations Convention on the Rights of the Child, it permits a traditional system like Trokosi to thrive. For instance, uprooting children from their parents and communities contravenes Article 8 and 9 of the United Nations Convention on the Rights of the Child. Article 8 (1) states: "States Parties undertake to respect the right of the child to preserve his or her identity, including nationality, name and family relations as recognized by law without unlawful interference." Separating young girls from their parents also contravenes Article 9 (1) which states:

> States Parties shall ensure that a child shall not be separated from his or her parents against their will, except when competent authorities subject to judicial review determine, in accordance with applicable law and procedures, that such separation is necessary for the best interests of the child...

It is also worthy of mention here that when girls are sent into Trokosi slavery, their original names are changed and they are given shrine names instead. This practice of changing the identity of girls sent into Trokosi servitude also contravenes Article 8 stated earlier on and also Article 7 which states: "The child shall be registered immediately after birth and shall have the right from birth to a name, the right to acquire a nationality, and as far as possible, the right to know and be cared for by her parents."

Committal of young virgin girls into Trokosi slavery against their consent also contravenes Article 12 (1) of the United Nations Child Rights Convention stating:

> States Parties shall assure to the child who is capable of forming his or her own views the right to express those views freely in all matters affecting the child, the views of the child being given due weight in accordance with the age and maturity of the child.

In addition, Article 16 unequivocally states: "No child shall be subjected to arbitrary or unlawful interference with his or her privacy, family, home or correspondence, nor unlawful attacks on his or her honor and reputation."

To the extent that girls enslaved in Trokosi practice are sexually assaulted resulting in physical, emotional and psychological trauma, the practice violates Article 12 (2) of the Ghana Constitution which provides: "All customary practices which dehumanize or are injurious to the physical and mental well-being of a person are prohibited." Further sexual abuse and exploitation are prohibited under Article 27 (1) of the United Nations African Charter on the Child and Article 19 and 34 of the Convention on the Rights of the Child which impose an obligation on states "to undertake to protect the child from all forms of sexual exploitation and sexual abuse."

The denial of Trokosi girls and their children the right to formal education violates Article 25 (1) of the Constitution of Ghana which states: "All persons shall have the right to equal education opportunities and facilities." Article 28 (4) of the Ghanaian Constitution asserts: "No child shall be deprived by any other person of medical treatment, education or any other social or economic benefit by reason only of religious or other beliefs." Furthermore, the right of the child to education is also spelt out in Article 11 (1) of the Draft Charter on the Rights and Welfare of the African Child and Article 28 (1) of the United Nations Convention on the Rights of the Child.

Indeed, we have witnessed young Trokosi girls of school age working on rice farms and engaged in heavy manual labor. This exploitation contravenes Article 32 (1) of the United Nations Convention of the Rights of the Child, which states:

> States Parties recognize the right of the child to be protected
> from economic exploitation and from performing any work

that is likely to be hazardous or to interfere with the child's education, or to be harmful to the child's health or physical, mental, spiritual, moral or social development.

In addition, The United Nations Conference on Women (the Beijing Conference, 1995) stressed the value of the girl child intimating that the skills, ideas, and energy of the girl child, woman of tomorrow, are vital for full attainment of the goals of equality, development, and peace. For the girl child to develop her full potential she needs to be nurtured in an enabling environment, where her spiritual, intellectual and material needs for survival are addressed.

Trokosi and Patriarchy

The practice of Trokosi violates the norms of the matrilineal system since it privileges male dominance and treats females as objects. Patriarchy regards males as central for the defense of the traditional society, so that in terms of decision making, patriarchal societies tend to marginalize the role of females.

Trokosi shrines are composed of mud houses and a compound fenced with palm branches. A Trokosi who decides that she will not be a part of the system can simply walk away. However, incarcerated Trokosi girls do not escape and spend their entire lives in servitude. The key to this puzzle lies in the social organization prevalent among most sub-Saharan African societies. It is the social organization of patriarchy, a system in which a male (known as the patriarch) acts as head of the family/household, holding power over females and children.

Patriarchy is from the Greek word "patér," genitive form "patris," with the root form "patr"- meaning father; and "arché" meaning old, beginning or, metaphorically, rule. The word is used to describe the cultural expectation that fathers have primary responsibility for the welfare of families (in ancient cultures, this included management of household slaves). The word is often used, by extension, to refer to societies where men are also expected to take primary responsibility for the welfare of the community as a whole, and take on the duties of public office (Essortment, 2009).

Patriarchy can also be defined as a social organization that structures the dominance of men over women. The power wielded by males in a patriarchal society can be defined in the Weberian sense to mean "the ability of persons or groups to command compliance from other persons or groups, even in the face of opposition" (Chafetz, 1990, p. 32). Chafetz (1990) also defines the authority or legitimacy to use the power from a Weberian sense to refer to "a perception on the part of both the power wielder and the complier that the former has the right to make binding decisions or issue commands, and the latter, the moral obligation to comply with them" (p. 32).

Most of the wrongs/crimes for which virgin girls are sent into servitude are committed by men. In addition, male family elders choose which girl has to go into servitude to atone for the crime of a family member. This decision is arrived at without consultation with or the consent of the girl. As Gadzekpo (1993) states, "Trokosi is an archaic and harsh justice system where mostly male criminals pay for their crime by offering up a usually female family member to serve the gods" (p. 5).

The system of patriarchy extends into the Trokosi shrines. Most of these shrines are owned by families with males sitting on the council of elders; a male priest performs the ritual and day-to-day administrative duties in the shrine. The priest is mostly assisted in his ritualistic duties by male devotees. The Trokosi girls are expected to serve and submit to these men totally. This fact is confirmed by Nukunya and Kwafo (1999a) who noted:

Total obedience is required by the Trokosi. She has to show this in the way she addresses and greets the priest and other functionaries. For instance, when handing over anything such as drinking water to them she has to go down on her knees; on no account or occasion should she refuse to carry out any order. (p. 26)

The power of patriarchy is also felt in the area of the sexual exploitation of the Trokosi girls. Obeying the orders of the priest includes having sexual intercourse with him at his pleasure. In addition, it entails becoming the sexual partner of male devotees. In confirming this fact Nukunya and Kwafo (1999a) state:

A lot is often said about the priest's easy sexual access to the Kosis [slaves]. This has been confirmed by the priests, the ritual functionaries and all Kosis old enough to have sex; though all functionaries as well as the priests are entitled to this privilege, it is the priest who has to make his intention felt in each case. (p. 26)

The power the priests have over the Trokosis is far reaching to the effect that even when released from the precinct of the shrine, the Trokosis are still fully committed sexually to the god and the priest who is the proxy husband. This situation has prevented released Trokosis from finding spouses from within their locality (Dovlo & Adzoyi, 1995).

As mentioned earlier, the Trokosi system is organized in such a way that the cycle of domination is perpetual. In most situations, young girls are sent to replace deceased Trokosi women, a clear miscarriage of justice, the reasons for the continuation are strategic, in that a mechanism is put in place to ensure economic, social, and political sustainability of the Trokosi system. The younger the Trokosi girls, the more strength they have to perform the many hours of labor needed on the farms of the

Trokosi priests. The turnover of new Trokosi girls provides a constant source of sexual gratification for male devotees and, subsequently, their allegiance to the shrine. This in turn provides a steady source of devotees and continuing political power for the priest.

Social and Legal Aspects of the Trokosi system

The process of presentation of virgins who become Trokosis amounts to setting up a criminal justice system that is an affront to the constitutional legal system guaranteed by the 1992 Constitution of Ghana (Short, 2001). When someone becomes a victim of a crime, that person consults at the shrine and promises that when the perpetrator is discovered he or she will be made to atone the gods with a virgin. The consequences of the invocations leading to serious catastrophe and death are not only cruel but also subversive of "rule of law" (Boateng, 2001). Further, the practice contravenes the basic human rights enshrined in the 1992 Constitution of Ghana. Article 26 (2), which prohibits all customary practices that dehumanize or are injurious to the physical and mental well being of Ghanaian citizens (Constitution of Ghana, 1992).

The system works within the context of a community's search for justice, but also under the authority of religion. A person who was a victim of a crime, or who has been offended by another, particularly when the culprit is unknown, would seek redress or vengeance through the gods at a shrine. The offended person approaches the custodian of the gods who invokes curses on the culprit. Such curses are believed to be effective, evidenced by mysterious deaths, a series of misfortunes, and illnesses in the family of the offender.

The causes of the affliction would normally be revealed following enquiries at the shrine. It is when families go to enquire about the meanings of calamities that have come upon them that they are given the facts regarding the offenses committed by a member of one family against another. The afflicted family, following the explanation of their misfortune, would submit a virgin to the shrine as part of the ritual process for the reversal of their problems. As tabooed persons, Trokosi women then go to live in the Troxovi shrines as consorts of the gods, and, by extension, wives of the traditional priests, who are the custodians of the shrines. In most of these shrines, once a person became a Trokosi, she remains virtually irredeemable. There are beliefs held that the descendants of the Trokosis are people who are destined to redeem their relatives from various crimes, despite the fact that the practice has commonly resulted in exploitation and sexual abuse of young girls. The practice is a source of controversy in Ghana, Togo, and Benin. But many pro-Trokosi academicians argue that the practice needs to be preserved with few modifications (Dartey-Kumodzi, 1995). In contrast, many social workers, human rights activists and NGOs are against the practice, and vigorously lobbied for its abolition in 1998, when the legislative Assembly promulgated a law to put a stop to the system (Ben-Ari, 2001).

CONCLUSION

Although human rights norms have been declared inalienable from a person's humanity by the international community, and most of these human rights standards have been incorporated into national constitutions and local laws, we still struggle to have these norms accepted, especially in traditional societies. The case of the Trokosi system among the Ewes and Dangmes in Ghana is an example of this phenomenon. While entrenched values, such as patriarchy and gender inequality, provide barriers to assimilation of human rights norms in traditional societies, the cultural relativism argument simply exacerbates the already intractable issue.

Trokosi as a patriarchal institution is a system of domination and economic exploitation of vulnerable children and women by men.

The exploitative tendencies of the Trokosi system have created a class society of male "haves" and female "have-nots" in Trokosi-practicing communities. In the name of religion and culture, the Trokosi system has kept thousands of women in fear and abject poverty, denied of their fundamental rights and freedoms while their male counterparts live in relative peace and contentment.

Furthermore, most of these young Trokosis are abused by the priests of the shrines because they do not have the power to resist the authority of these men. The girls are taken out of school and sent into servitude as Trokosis (Ahiable, 1995). However, the original children of these priests are sent to formal schools.

In order to completely eradicate dehumanizing cultural practices such as Trokosi, we need to break down the barriers of patriarchy and gender inequality. This can be done through incorporating issues of gender equality, and human rights, women's rights and children's rights in school curriculum beginning in kindergarten, through to tertiary institutions. Those who do not have the benefit of formal education should be targeted through sustained adult literacy and community awareness programs. The National Commission on Civic Education, the Commission on Human Rights, and the Ghana Education Service, for example, can carry out this mandate. NGOs can also join in the campaign.

Flagrant violations of human rights such as those inherent in the Trokosi system must not be allowed to persist without decisive action from government and law enforcement agencies. Beyond educating community members about the evils of the practice, and employing moral persuasion to stop it, perpetrators must be brought to justice so that their punishment can serve as a deterrent to others. As the maxim goes "justice delayed is justice denied." Those who hide behind the cloak of cultural relativism to openly promote human rights abuses, as in the case of the Trokosi practice, should be considered accomplices and dealt with according to law. In the case of Ghana, the criminal law against customary servitude must be enforced to the letter and violators persecuted. By so doing, the government of Ghana will be given teeth to Article 32 (2) of the United Nations Convention on the Rights of the Child which states that States Parties shall take legislative, administrative, social and educational measures to ensure the implementation of the present article. To this end, and having regard to the relevant provisions of other international instruments, States Parties shall in particular:

(a) Provide for a minimum age or minimum ages for admission to employment;

(b) Provide for appropriate regulation of the hours and conditions of employment;

(c) Provide for appropriate penalties or other sanctions to ensure the effective enforcement of the present article.

The international community, especially bilateral and multilateral aid agencies and financial institutions, should continue to move away from political rhetoric and intensify the need for democracy, good governance, and sustained human rights records, as necessary preconditions for aid and financial assistance.

Finally, every effort must be made to rehabilitate women and children incarcerated in the Trokosi system. All victims must be provided with psychosocial and emotional counseling to help deal with their traumatic experiences. Women victims should be provided with vocational skills and training to ensure their economic integration into society. Children should be provided with opportunities such as scholarships, and educational materials to help them go back to school.

REFERENCES

Abotchie, C. (1997a). Legal processes and institution. In F. Agbodeka (Ed.), *A handbook of Eweland. Volume I: The Ewes of southeastern Ghana* (pp. 63-89). Accra, Ghana: Woeli Publishing Services.

Abotchie, C. (1997b). *Social control in traditional southern Eweland of Ghana*. Accra, Ghana: Ghana University Press.

Amenumey, D. E. K. (1997). A brief history. In F. Agbodeka (Ed.), *A handbook of Eweland. Volume I: The Ewes of southeastern Ghana* (pp. 14-27). Accra, Ghana: Woeli Publishing Services.

Ahiable, M. (1995). *The anatomy of Trokosi system in Ghana*. Paper presented at the First National Workshop on Trokosi System, Accra, Ghana.

Amnesty International. (2002). Pakistan: The tribal justice system in Pakistan.

Retrieved August 29, 2008, from http://asiapacific.amnesty.org/library/Index/ENGASA330242002?open&of=ENG-2AS

An-na'im, A. A., & Deng, F. M. (1990). *Human rights in Africa: Cross cultural perspectives.* Washington, DC: Brookings Institution.

Beijing Declaration and Platform for Action. (1995, September). Fourth World

Conference on Women, 15 September 1995, A/CONF.177/20 (1995) and A/CONF.177/20/Add.1 (1995). University of Minnesota Human Rights Library. Retrieved August 29, 2008, from http://www1.umn.edu/humanrts/instree/e5dplw.htm

Ben-Ari, N. (2001). Liberating girls from 'Trokosi': Campaign against ritual servitude in Ghana. *African Recovery, 15*(4), 26-27.

Boateng, A. (2001). *The Trokosi system in Ghana: African women and children.* Westport, CT: Westport Praeger.

Boateng, A. B. (1995). *The chief as a tool for change in the Trokosi system.* Paper presented at the First National Workshop on Trokosi System, Accra, Ghana.

Boateng, N. A. (2004). *Traditional governance from the Queen Mother's perspective.* Lecture given at the International Conference on Chieftaincy in Africa: Culture, Governance, and Development, Accra, Ghana.

Brown, J. M. (1989). *Gandhi: Prisoner of hope.* London. Yale University Press.

Burn, S. M. (2005). *Women across cultures: A global perspective.* New York: McGraw-Hill.

Campbell, G., Miers, S., & Miller, J. C. (2008). *Women and slavery: Africa, the Indian Ocean world, and the medieval North Atlantic.* Athens, OH: Ohio University Press.

Chafetz, J. J. (1990). *Gender equity: An integrated theory of stability and change.* Newbury Park, CA: Sage Publications.

Cohen, J., & Arator, A. (1992). *Political theory and civil society.* Cambridge: MIT Press.

Criminal Code (Amendment) Act of the Republic of Ghana. (1998). *Act 554.* Accra, Ghana: State Publishing.

Dartey-Kumodzi, S. (1995). Trokosi or fiashidi: Pillar of Africa's survival. *Weekly Spectator,* July 15, 5.

DAWN. (2003, June 6). Victim of "Swara" custom acquitted: Sentence in murder case overturned. Retrieved August 29, 2008, from http://www.dawn.com/2003/06/06/local28.htm

Deann, A. (2005). Sex slaves' slow freedom: Sometimes it takes years to negotiate their release. *Christianity Today, 49*(2), 22-22.

Dovlo, E., & Adzoyi, K. A. (1995). Report on Trokosi institution. *Report on Trokosi institution.* Accra, Ghana: International Needs.

Dovlo, E., & Kufogbe, S. K. (1997). *Baseline survey on female ritual bondage in Ghana: The geographical spread and count of victims: Phase I, southern Ghana.* Accra, Ghana. International Needs Ghana and CIDA.

Dwamena-Aboagye, A. (2002). Women working to make a difference. *Human Rights: Journal of the Section of Individual Rights & Responsibilities, 29*(3), 22-23.

Every Child Minisries. (n.d.). Modern-day slavery: "Trokosi" slave children in Africa. Retrieved September 30, 2009, from http://www.ecmafrica.org/page.aspx?id=36223

Essortment. (2009). What is Patriarchy? Retrieved October 1, 2009, from http://www.essortment.com/all/whatispatriarc_rhsf.htm

Fennis, J. (1990). *International human rights: Universalism v. relativism.* Newbury Park, CA: Sage Publications. First West African Sub-Regional Workshop on Female Ritual Servitude. (2001, February). *Harnessing our collective resources for the transformation of ritual servitude.* Accra, Ghana: ING.

Gadzekpo, A. (1993). Sexual bondage. *Awo Magazine, 5,* 5-7.

Ghana Home Page. (2009). Geography. Retrieved September 30, 2009, from http://ghanaweb.com/GhanaHomePage/geography/

Ghana Home Page. (2009). Maps of Ghana: Major cities. Retrieved May 27, 2008, from www.ghanaweb.com/imagelib/dest/12307026.gif

Goldtzamann, J. C. (1998). Cultural relativity or cultural intrusion? Female ritual slave in Western Africa and the international covenant on civil and political rights: Ghana as a case study. *New England International and Comparative Law Annual, 4,* 53-72.

Adokuwa, IV., M. A. (1995, July). *The role of queen mothers in bringing change in Trokosi system in Ghana.* A paper presented at International Needs workshop, Accra, Ghana.

Mazrui, A. A., Ajayi, J. F. A., Boahen, A. A., & Tshibangu, T. (1993). Trends in philosophy and science in Africa. In A. A. Mazrui

(Ed.), *General history of Africa: Vol. 8. Africa since 1935* (pp. 633-677). France: UNESCO publication chapter.

Mendosa, E. L. (2002). *West Africa: An introduction to its history, civilization and contemporary situation.* Durham, NC: Carolina Academic Press. Memorandum from Chiefs. (1991). [Restitution for Trokosi victims submitted to the north Tongu district assembly]. Unpublished raw data.

Miers, S., & Klein, M. (1999). *Slavery and colonial rule in Africa.* London: Frank Cass National Archives of Ghana. (ADM. 11/ 568, ADM. 11/768).

Naidoo K., & Tandon, R. (1999). The promise of civil society. In K. Naidoo (Ed.), *Civil society at the Millennium* (pp. 1-16). West Hartford, CT: Kumarian Press.

[National Archives of Ghana?]. [ca. 1920]. *The Trokosi System* [Complaints about Human Rights Abuses in Colonial Ghana] *ADM.11/568,* ADM.11/768. Accra, Ghana: National Archives.

New International Version (NIV) Bible. (1984). Deuteronomy 5:9 NIV. Retrieved September 30, 2009, from http://www.biblica.com/ bible/verse/index.php?q=ezekiel18:2&niv=yes

New International Version (NIV) Bible. (1984). Exodus 20:5 NIV. Retrieved September 30, 2009, from http://www.biblica.com/ bible/verse/index.php?q=ezekiel18:2&niv=yes

New International Version (NIV) Bible. (1984). Exodus 34:7 NIV. Retrieved September 30, 2009, from http://www.biblica.com/ bible/verse/index.php?q=ezekiel18:2&niv=yes

New International Version (NIV) Bible. (1984). Ezekiel 18:2 NIV. Retrieved September 30, 2009, from http://www.biblica.com/ bible/verse/index.php?q=ezekiel18:2&niv=yes

New International Version (NIV) Bible. (1984). Jeremiah 31:29 NIV. Retrieved September 30, 2009, from http://www.biblica.com/ bible/verse/index.php?q=jeremiah31:29&niv=yes

New International Version (NIV) Bible. (1984). Numbers 14:18 NIV. Retrieved September 30, 2009, from http://www.biblica.com/ bible/verse/index.php?q=jeremiah31:29&niv=yes

Nikolić-Ristanović, V. (2000). *Women, violence and war: Wartime victimization of refugees in the Balkans.* Hungary: Central European University Press.

Nukunya, G. K. (1997a). Festivals. In F. Adegboka (Ed.), *A handbook of Eweland, Volume I: The Ewes of southeastern Ghana* (pp. 24-40). Accra, Ghana: Woeli Publishing Services.

Nukunya, G. K. (1997b). The land and the people. In F. Agbodeka (Ed.), *A handbook of Eweland, Volume I: The Ewes of southeastern Ghana* (pp. 3-18). Accra, Ghana: Woeli Publishing Services.

Nukunya, G. K. (1997c). Social and political institutions. In F. Agbodeka (Ed.), *A handbook of Eweland, Volume I: The Ewes of southeastern Ghana* (pp. 47-55). Accra, Ghana: Woeli Publishing Services.

Nukunya, G. K., & Kwafo, S. K. (1999a). *Report on de-criminalizing Trokosi: A research into the nature and operations of ritual enslavement in south eastern Ghana.* Accra, Ghana: International Needs.

Nukunya, G. K., & Kwafo, S. K. (1999b). *Report on the Trokosi system in south eastern Ghana*. Accra, Ghana: International Needs.

Office of the High Commissioner for Human Rights. (1989). *Convention on the Rights of the Child*. Retrieved February 25, 2005, from http://www.unhchr.ch/html/menu3/b/k2crc.htm

Reagan, T. (1999). *Non-western educational traditions. Alternative approaches to educational thought and practice*. Mahiwah, NJ: Lawrence Erlbaum Associates.

Resolution of Tongu paramount chiefs and queenmothers. (1991, August). *1st National Workshop on Female Ritual Servitude*. Accra, Ghana.

Rojas, O. (1999). The role of civil society organizations in sustainable development. In K. Naidoo (Ed.), *Civil society at the Millennium* (pp. 85-96). West Hartford, CT: Kumarian Press.

Romanoff, D. (1999). *Trokosi in Klikor, Ghana*. Unpublished undergraduate research project, University of Montana, Missoula.

Sadik, N. (1995). *Madam president, honorable delegates*. Paper presented at the Fourth

World Conference on Women, Beijing, China. Retrieved August 29, 2008 from http://www.un.org/esa/gopherdata/conf/fwcw/conf/una/950905174345.txt

Second National Workshop on Trokosi System in Ghana. (1998, April). *Report of the Second National Workshop on Trokosi System in Ghana: Securing the inalienable rights of women and children in Trokosi bondage*. Accra, Ghana: British Council.

Short, E. (2001, February). *Harmonizing the laws and programs to eradicate servitude in the West African sub-region.* Speech presented at the 1st West African Sub-Regional Workshop on Female Ritual Servitude, Accra, Ghana.

Sowah, C. W. (1993). *The Tongu in search of unity.* Unpublished master's thesis, University of Ghana, Accra, Ghana.

Symonides, J. (2002). *Human rights: Concepts and standards* (Ed.). Dartmouth Publishing.

The Republic of Ghana. (1992). *Constitution of the Republic of Ghana.* Tema, Ghana: Ghana Publishing Corporation.

United Nations. (1995). *United Nations conference on women: The Beijing conference.* New York: United Nations.

United States Department of State. (2009). International religious freedom report 2002: Ghana. Retrieved September 30, 2009, from http://www.state.gov/g/drl/rls/irf/2002/13835.htm

Westermann, D. (1935). Mitteilung des Seminars fir Ori- entalische Sprachen an der Universitat Berlin [Report on the workshop on Asian languages at the University of Berlin]. *Die Glidji Ewe in Togo, Beiband zum Jahrgang, 38,* 253-254.

Wiafe, S. (2000). Slaves of tradition: Fetish priests are targets of campaign in Ghana. *New Internationalist, 10*(328), 19-28.

ABOUT THE AUTHORS

 **WISDOM MENSAH** WAS BORN IN Denu in the Volta Region of Ghana. He had his primary and middle school education in his hometown. He took his GCE ordinary level in Keta Business Secondary School and Advanced level in Tema Secondary School. He served a mandatory one-year national service by working with the National Savings and Credit Bank and then proceeded to the University of Ghana at Legon in 1985 to pursue a three-year Bachelor of Arts degree program in Law and Sociology.

In September 1989, Wisdom joined International Needs Ghana, a non-governmental, not-for-profit and humanitarian organization as a project officer. Being the pioneer staff of this newly established organization, Wisdom had the rare privilege of working at all levels of the organization – as messenger, secretary, accounts officer, purchasing/procurement officer, administrative officer, projects coordinator and acting executive director. From 1990 to 2003, he coordinated the Trokosi Modernization Program, a multi-million-dollar advocacy and rehabilitation program aimed at the emancipation and reintegration into society of thousands of girls enslaved in ritual cult servitude. His outstanding leadership and negotiation skills contributed in great measure to the emancipation of over 3,000 Trokosi women and several hundreds of their children from servitude.

Wisdom currently holds a Ph.D. in Cultural Studies in Education from Ohio University, U.S.A. He earned a Master of Arts degree in Public Administration (MPA) also from Ohio University; a Bachelor of Arts degree in Law and Sociology from the University of Ghana, Legon; a certificate in Project Planning and Management from Ghana Institute of Management, Productivity and Administration (GIMPA) in 1994; a Post-graduate Diploma in NGO Management from Aarhus School of Architecture in Denmark in 1999; and a Certificate in Management of Development Organizations from Coady International Institute of St. Francis Xavier University in Antigonish, Canada in 2002.

FRANCIS E. GODWYLL IS AN Assistant Professor and currently the program Coordinator of Cultural Studies in Education at Ohio University. He obtained his Ph.D. in Education from the University of Education in Heidelberg, Germany after having studied for his Masters in Education and a Bachelor's honors degree in Education at the University of Cape Coast, Ghana. He additionally holds a Diploma in Religions (equivalent of Associate Degree).

Francis has 16 years of university teaching experience, was a Lecturer in Education at the University of Cape Coast and also an adjunct faculty for the University of Education at Winneba, Ghana. Before joining Ohio University, Francis Godwyll worked as an adjunct faculty for MED students pursuing Interdisciplinary Studies in Curriculum and Instruction an MED Field-Based Program at the International Campus of the National-Louis University Heidelberg and the *Institut für Heilpedagogie* in Schlierbach, Germany. He also worked collaboratively with educational administrators, policy makers, international donor agencies, parents, community leaders and local educational supervisors. He has immense experience in school-age programs for students with and without disabilities and been involved in evaluation and certification of student-teachers and teachers of K-12 throughout Ghana in both regular and special schools.

He served as a consultant on educational policy, reform issues and program monitoring/evaluation for the Ministry of Education in Ghana, SOS Village School Projects in Ghana (a private welfare organization catering for orphaned and destitute children) and the Ghana National Association of Teachers (GNAT).

Awards received include: Ohio University College of Education Distinguished Graduate Teaching Award in 2009 and 2006; award for teaching excellence by the Chair of Educational Studies Department in 2004; a highly competitive scholarship for doctoral studies by the German Academic Exchange Service (Deutscher Akademischer Austausschdienst - DAAD) in 1997-2001.

Books authored and coauthored include *Fundamentals of Special Education, Games for Learning in School and at Home, Diagnostically Supported Teaching Strategies to Reduce School Failure, Poverty, Education and Development* among others. He has also authored book chapters, articles and presented at national and international conferences.

His research interests broadly falls under marginalized populations and the use of education as a tool for empowerment encompassing but not limited to poverty, education and sustainable development, HIV/AIDS, gender issues, the African child, children's rights & communication barriers, early childhood philosophies and practices, diversity and equity issues, language as a tool for social mobility, local knowledge utilization, globalization and ICT.

INDEX

79, 80, 81, 82, 85, 86, 93,
  94, 95, 96, 100
Human Rights Advocacy and
  Education 47

I

Identity 32, 36, 42, 88
Incarcerated in the shrine 3
Initial intervention strategy 48
Inmates of the shrines 16
Innocent children 16
International viii, xii, xiv, 5, 15,
  33, 34, 35, 36, 46, 47, 48,
  55, 56, 59, 60, 64, 65, 68,
  69, 74, 75, 76, 82, 97, 98,
  99, 100, 101, 102, 103,
  104, 105, 106
International advocacy 56
International community 75, 79,
  94, 96
International development 75
International Needs Ghana
  (ING) 47, 74

J

Justice xii, 24, 76, 80, 84, 91, 92,
  93, 95, 97
Justice delayed 95
Justice denied 95

K

Kaja shrine 39
Kosis 92

L

Libation 8, 73
Liberation 5, 14, 44, 46, 54, 75
Lineage 22, 23, 24, 25
Lineage membership 24

Local 5, 15, 42, 50, 53, 56, 57,
  60, 62, 72, 74, 77, 94, 107

M

Mande 17
Manual labor 43, 85, 89
Maternal 7, 9
Matrilineal 39, 90
Matrilineal system 39, 90
Medical care 4, 13, 82
Medicine drinking shrines 39
Menstruation 4, 13, 14, 85, 87
Microcredit programs 75
Minerals 20
Miscarriage of justice 92
Missionaries 45
Missions international 46, 75
Moral persuasion 95
Moral values 42

N

National Commission on Civic
  Education 53, 73, 76, 95
NGO's (International Govern-
  mental Organizations) 74
North Tonga District Admin-
  istrations 29, 37, 40, 44,
  47, 48, 49, 51, 53, 73
Nutritious food 4

O

Objects of reparation 55, 84
Offender 25, 93
Oral tradition 28, 29
Organization 30
Organizational structure 23, 30

P

Paternal 9, 32

Twisted

Tales

Flash Fiction with a Twist
2013

Edited by

Annie Evett and Margie Riley

Raging Aardvark Publishing